OVERTHINKING

AND

MASTER YOUR EMOTIONS

Find Out All the Innovative Secrets to Illuminate Your Mental Strength, Empower Your Self-Esteem, Destroy Anxiety, Procrastination, and Negative Thoughts

Laurance Rosemberg, Silvia Watson

© **Copyright 2020 by Laurance Rosemberg - All rights reserved.**

The content within this book may not be reproduced, duplicated or transmitted without direct written permission from the author or the publisher. Under no circumstances will any blame or legal responsibility be held against the publisher, or author, for any damages, reparation, or monetary loss due to the information contained within this book. Either directly or indirectly.

Legal Notice:

This book is copyright protected. This book is only for personal use. You cannot amend, distribute, sell, use, quote or paraphrase any part, or the content within this book, without the consent of the author or publisher.

Disclaimer Notice:

Please note the information contained within this document is for educational and entertainment purpose only. All effort has been executed to present accurate, up to date, and reliable, complete information. No warranties of any kind are declared or implied. Readers acknowledge that the author is not engaging in the rendering of legal, financial, medical or professional advice. The content within this book has been derived from various sources. Please consult a licensed professional before attempting any techniques outlined in this book.
By reading this document, the reader agrees that under no circumstances is the author responsible for any losses, direct or indirect, which are incurred as a result of the use of information

contained within this document, including, but not limited to, errors, omissions, or inaccuracies.

Table of Contents

Introduction 1

Chapter 1: The Danger of Overthinking 4

Chapter 2: Suggestions to Unlock Your Mental Potential 11

Chapter 3: Going Through Your Past to Improve Your Future. 22

Chapter 4: Stoic and Mindfulness Techniques to Leave Some Space for Useful Thoughts 28

    1) Pay Attention to the Rhythm of Your Breath.................. 32

    2) Pay Attention to Your Posture... 33

    3) Control the Music That Controls You............................ 33

    4) Place a Hand Lens on the Present 34

Chapter 5: How to Practice Mental Minimalism 35

    1) Think about Two Objects That You Don't Use Anymore but That You've Never Thrown Away Because You Felt Somehow Affectionate 36

    2) Don't Look for The Support of Other Minimalists. Don't Look for Approval, Don't Try to Enter Groups of People Who Practice Minimalism 37

    3) Remember: Collateral Events Are Just Temporary 37

    4) Project Yourself in the Future of Filling 37

    5) Did You Know That Self-Realization Can't Happen Without the Emotional Impulse Towards the Other? 38

    6) Understand the Reasons Why You Are Hesitant to Get Rid of Certain Objects 38

Chapter 6: 10 Suggestions to Immediately Improve Your Life . 40

    1) Stay Away from People Who Bother Your Mental Health 40

2) Try to Reduce Sugars 41

3) Throw Your TV from Your Balcony (But Make Sure Nobody's Underneath!) 41

4) Become the Conductor of Relationships, Not the Chaser 42

5) Reduce Your Use of the Mobile Phone 43

6) Don't Compare Your Life to Others' Lives 43

7) One Goal at a Time 44

8) The Past Is Just a Lesson to Let Us Understand What Went Wrong 44

9) Reduce Social Networks and News, Because You Don't Need Them (If The End of the World's Coming, Someone Will Warn You!) 45

10) Be Present and Follow Your Dreams, Instead of Focusing On Others' Dreams 46

Chapter 7: Find Out How to Win Over Indecision.................... 47

Chapter 8: Find Out How to Win Over Procrastination 53

Chapter 9: Ideal Zen Meditation That Will Make You a Better Person... 59

    What is FA Meditation? 59

    What's the DMN? 60

    The Space of Action That You Subtract from Your Ego Will Be Filled from the Action of Awareness 62

Chapter 10: Guide to Improve Your Life in 21 Days 65

    My Words Are Not Here to Tell You Who You Are, But to Remind You Who You Are 75

    The Ability to Control Accidental Events That Claim to Control Us 80

    How Many Times Have You Not Been a Caring Father to Your Body? 91

The Source of All the Possible Meanings Is Also the Source of All Possible Solutions 93

The Functioning of Your Organs Comes from Absolute Perfection 94

Self-Analysis Means Freeing Oneself from Others' Interpretations 96

Chapter 11: A first Overview of Emotions................................ 110

Chapter 12: What Does Science Say About Emotions?............ 115

Chapter 13: Definitions, Interpretations, and Misinterpretations of the Ego...120

Chapter 14: How Do Words Impact Emotions? 127

Chapter 15: How Does the Environment Impact Your Emotions? 135

Chapter 16: How Do Emotions Form? 140

Chapter 17: Emotions Can Be the Compass Guiding Your Path 145

Chapter 18: How Emotion Can Help Us in Our Personal Growth 150

Chapter 19: How to Align the Logical and Emotional Sphere.. 157

Chapter 20: What Is and How Do We Improve Emotional Intelligence 162

Chapter 21: Learning How to Know Oneself to Understand Where Emotions Come From 184

Chapter 22: How to Use the Jedi Method to Master Your Inner Self...189

Chapter 23: Theories and Practices to Win Resentment, Performance Anxiety, Fear, Procrastination, and jealousy...... 196

Chapter 24: Learn the Art of Detachment................................ 202

Chapter 25: 21 Days to Get to Master Your Emotions 204

Introduction

Truth flows and dies in the thought because every thought-truth already leads to the destruction of the intuited-truth.

The heavier the overload of thought, the heavier the burden of destruction.

When you think too much, something mysterious overturns the events: you're thought by your thought.

You become the passive spectator of your relentless active being. A lumbering thought becomes the actor who steals your part in a theatre piece, and you become its fading doubling: something that follows its movements, step after step, word after word, image after image.

You become the accidental imitation of your thought, which is superb, vain, egocentric, and asks the world to revolve around itself. And it actually happens. Everything starts turning around the lumbering thought.

Even the clock hands rotate around it because the lumbering thought feeds itself of your time.

You need to take back the throne you're entitled to have. You're not here to live in subjection. You're too talented to accept the role of a body double, do you get it?

You think you're the one to give orders to your thoughts, right? And yet, it rolls you up, it engulfs you like a matryoshka, it shakes you, it makes you whirl around, it clouds your brain and leaves you at the mercy of its repetitive movement.

You know, if you look ahead, even if for just a minute, you can see the leftovers of its dictatorship. You can see the traces of the overthinking's dictatorship. Look in front of yourself. It left a lot of fog on the windshield of your performance. And there's a talking rearview mirror, who's looking at you, and saying: stop, please! you're still in time to stop!

Here it is, the machine of your creativity is rebelling against the thought's overload.

If you can't stop on purpose, sooner or later your unconscious will make you accidentally clash, because it will be the only way to slow the race down.

And you don't want to clash, do you?

You don't want to find yourself full of psychosomatic symptoms, which are the signs of the clashes decided by your unconscious behind your back. No, you don't want it.

But there's only one way to avoid the clash: becoming your thought's owner.

Let your conscience do, according to your will, what your unconscious might be forced to do without your will.

The unconscious is as severe as it is self-sufficient and never asks permission to act.

It fills itself with poison, overflows with it, and then explodes. And you're about to explode. Then you find yourself drowning in your own poison, looking everywhere for the culprit.

You won't see that the guilty part is inside of you, and it also has a name: overthinking.

Do you know what's the worst thing about people with too much fantasy? They manage to create their happiness with the same strength with which they create their pain.

Well, you're now in front of the devastating power of overthinking.

What do you want to do?

Chapter 1: The Danger of Overthinking

How can a lumbering thought be damaging for ourselves and our relationships?

Imagine having an objective. Fixed, firm, stable. Imagine that your objective is situated on the highest part of a rock. You greet your friends who are waiting for you down there, you climb, you wave, and you're breathless. You stop, take a deep breath, observe your objective carefully at the lenses, almost as if you were zooming with your eyes, so as not to lose sight of the precise point of your self-fulfillment.

Here it is. Imagine this is your path.

But suddenly, while you're concentrated, while your eyes are shining on the goal, a wave hits you, and then another one, and then another one, until a brutal and fierce storm starts stirring under you.

The worry-storm generates itself when your thoughts become overwhelming.

Waves hit you with unprecedented power, and you're afraid, sure you are, but fear created other intrusive thoughts, and this is how waves sum up, multiplicate, and the focus of the lens gradually becomes dimmer and dimmer, until you can hardly see it anymore, distracted by the noise of the waves and their incessant beating against your body.

The overload-storm could lead you to your fall and you could collapse any moment, even if you were just one step away from your goal.

People always told us that there's no way to stop the storm because it doesn't depend on us.

But what if I told you that this time the waves of the sea are going to follow your mental waves?

And what if I told you that waves only imitate your mind? What if I told you that this time you're not in the storm, but you're the storm itself?

To stop the storm, you have to stop yourself. You're not the victim, you're the storm's butcher.

Remember: you can be the creator, but you can even be a destructor. And you're a big creator, you're very talented at creating, your creativity is so strong that it can even create sophisticated monsters.

Nothing's over, as long as you have the possibility to win against the storm. But wait. You don't have to struggle to win. It won't be a battle. It doesn't have to be a battle. Fighting against yourself means infuriating the existing storm.

It only takes a strong blow to win it, so that it will go away. It's not necessary to punch it! It doesn't have to be a war, just an extraordinary, immense blow.

It is an act of abandonment. We will call it: the breath of abandonment.

Contraction and release. After blowing against the storm, after contracting your muscles to produce the breath, your body will automatically release, it will abandon itself.

Likewise, if your mind will be able to surrender to the confidence that your goal will be achieved even without constant brooding, the lumbering thought will be abandoned.

The breath of abandonment is not abandoning yourself completely and collapsing off the cliff. It is just surrendering to the power of the breath while remaining nailed to the rock.

A breath can move what a war can't move. And if you know where to look for air, if you know how to let yourself through the air, then you know where to take all the air needed to move an entire storm.

You should know one thing: overthinking is not only harmful to ourselves, but also to our relationships.

Chronic overthinking can be compared to chronic tinnitus.

Do you know the ringing in your ears?

In the beginning, as they come out, you notice them clearly. Of course, you notice them. You hear all the annoyance, the intrusion into silence, the distortion of the reality of sound, and then you get irritated, and you want to drive them out, dissipate them in some way.

But then something unexpected happens.

Tinnitus becomes so present, so constant, that it becomes your new silence.

You can no longer even imagine what the silence was like before it was occupied by tinnitus.

You forget how you were without tinnitus. The sound of life becomes a distortion. And the distortion becomes your new normality.

Well, this is what happens when overthinking becomes chronic. You don't even notice anymore. You're wrapped in your malaise, you're in it up to your neck.

But you can't see it, hear it, or touch it. Your mind welcomes its presence no longer because presence has now become coexistence.

And this is how you stop living and start coexisting. You don't realize it anymore, but your dizziness doesn't prevent overthinking from any more damage. The worst ones are the ones that don't send you any signal or notification; they're silent, insolent spites.

They climb the nets of your relationships, they corrupt them and break them, but you don't know it, and you only notice it when you're about to collapse, no longer supported by the net that was holding you up.

Thinking too many tears away the immediacy of your emotions. Any friendship, any affection, any love, sooner or later will shatter under the wheels of lumbering thoughts. Because you are no longer feeling, you're analyzing.

But are you aware that analysis—because of its cyclical formulation of questions, hypotheses, conjectures about the nature of emotions—creates an impoverishment of feelings?

Perhaps so. Perhaps you are aware of it. But this is not enough to stop your analytical obstinacy.

You tell yourself: "Well, that's who I am! What are you going to do about it?"

You tell yourself: "I think too much."

You justify yourself, you forgive yourself, or maybe you think you forgive yourself. And yet, I assure you, a part of you will not forgive you.

I'm talking about the part of yourself that wants to feel pure emotions, the uncontaminated ones, which are free to flow; that part will not forgive you the rain of analysis that you've dropped, the rain that has dampened the emotion, fading it, and then making it disappear.

Can you even imagine how many emotions you let unconsciously die?

You've circled around so much with your thoughts, with your doubts about their authenticity, that in the end, by dint of turning and turning, you generated a hurricane, and emotions were thrown away.

Remember what we said? The breath of abandonment.

Yes, the breath of abandonment can beat even the breath of the hurricane.

If you abandon yourself to emotions, emotions will sprout unhindered.

I know, thinking a lot has always been your most characterizing trait. Maybe it made you feel special, somehow. Having so many ideas seems to be much more attractive than having just one idea at a time.

But what if I told you that they all were useless ideas? And what if I told you that even in just one, single idea, one can concentrate the same intuitive strength that sums up a thousand different ideas?

Trust your only guessed intuition. Intuition does not need too many elaborations to emerge; it will come out as a memorable, light, spark in the moment of mental darkness.

Remember: your relationships will suffer from your overthinking. Overthinking in love becomes computing power, anxiety measurement, suspicion. Even the strongest love, sooner or later, will clash against the wall of calculus.

Calculus chases feelings, but feelings escape it. You know that perfectly.

And you also know that you continuously chase after calculus and feelings.

Well, don't be surprised if you find yourself exhausted, and don't be surprised if your partner will be exhausted as well.

Nobody can avoid the collateral effects of chasing and escaping. The problem needs to be eliminated at its roots.

There is no need to act on the effects of the malaise if you do nothing but crystallize the cause of the malaise.

There is no need to dab the pain if you continue to tear the wound.

You deserve to have happy relationships. Stop hiding under the carpet of misfortune, accident, bad luck.

Start getting rid of fragmented relationships, start getting rid of overthinking!

Chapter 2: Suggestions to Unlock Your Mental Potential

Maybe they already told you that you're brilliant. Or maybe nobody ever told you, and therefore, you think you aren't.

Let me unveil a secret: when a human being sees a shining object, only two reactions are contemplated. They could feel overwhelmed because the light might place them in front of his lack of light. In that case, they will stay silent. As an alternative, they could admire it, because they will recognize themselves in it. And they will stay silent even in that case.

Well, let's say that humans prefer to shut up, in front of brilliant people. So, don't be afraid. Don't think you're not brilliant just because nobody ever told you.

You're a shining light that scares people, or something that calms people, so much that it makes them stay silent, either because of turmoil or because of relaxation.

Trust me, a truly brilliant person doesn't need to hear it from others.

Have you ever seen a diamond stop being a diamond just because nobody caressed it?

Have you ever seen a star darken just because nobody praised it?

You don't really need to be caressed and praised to feel sure of your worth.

Your value doesn't need to be corroborated by the judgment of others. Remember: others' judgment is always imperfect because it is incomplete. No judgment is ever complete and accomplished. No judgment is ever absolute because the perspective of those who judge you are always partial.

Every judgment is formulated in a present time, based on the elements known in a present time. And it will be easy for you to understand that then, the judgment does not contemplate future transformations.

So, keep it in mind: the perspective of judgment is reduced both spatially and temporally.

And if you need to fit into an imperfect judgment to feel less imperfect, something is wrong. There is something out of tune in this need of yours. Do you get it?

If a judgement is imperfect in its nature, well, why do you think it could tell you if you are more or less perfect?

An imperfect could never tell you about perfection. And a dull human being could never talk about your lightness: they don't recognize it, because it doesn't know what it is.

Hence, you can't rely on the dark to certify light. No light could comfort you better than your own light, which is usually known but never recognized.

Yes, maybe your problem is not that you don't know, but that you don't recognize.

Maybe you've never looked in the mirror enough, looking for wonder. Maybe you've only used it to see your flaws, from the ill-concealed ones to those more deeply anchored to the invisible. You've drafted a list of your faults while you were standing in front of the mirror, looking for disharmony of forms, unconscious of the fine line that separates harmony from disharmony.

Do you know there'd be no disharmony if we had no desire for harmony? A flaw is not a mess, it's just a spark of a desiring tension.

If everything was harmonious, harmony would turn out to be the most boring event of the universe, because it'd be the only possible presence in every corner.

When something looks good, even the prettiest one, becomes overloading or invasive, we don't like it anymore.

Therefore, your flaws protect you from harmony's possibility to invade you.

And trust me: next time you'll be looking in the mirror, looking for some disharmonic points, stop the search. Get out of the habit, abandon the old search. Start a new search. This time look for your light.

When your eyes will be shining in the mirror, there you are: you have found your light.

You can finally tell yourself: I am a brilliant person. I am a brilliant person.

Do you see it? Sometimes it's enough to change the coordinates of a search, to find the real treasure you were looking for.

It's important for you to know that intelligent people have few relationships because they have a great talent in the work of selection. Intelligent people don't benefit from the company of just anyone. They want to be surrounded by people who can enrich them, who make them come out enriched, always.

And yes, intelligent people like you, are very afraid of impoverished people.

They are afraid of those people who always use the wrong words in the wrong place, impoverishing the language. They are afraid of those who always move the wrong accusation to the wrong culprit, impoverishing justice.

They are afraid of those who always throw the wrong weight to the wrong lightness, impoverishing the balance.

Selecting people is a form of safeguarding your inner baggage.

But keep in mind that sometimes, even rarely, you learn more from observing a mistake than from observing a right act.

It's as if the mistake pointed us down the wrong path, and we consequently sense the right path simply by reasoning in opposition.

In addition, intelligent people have a few relationships because they're focused on their goals. They feel all the suffocating burden of wasting time, wasting energy, wasting opportunities. In short, they have imagined all the danger that revolves around the waste.

You don't have to force yourself to hang out with a lot of people just because others want you to be more sociable.

Who the hell decided that someone has to decide for us?

And a lover of solitude is not a madman who wants to isolate himself from the world, damn it! He's just a lover of solitude; he's just in love with the most authentic treasure chest of art.

Because art is kept inside of you. And if you find the time to look inside of yourself, you find art.

There is a time to do, and there is a time to think.

There is a time to interact, and there is a time to reflect on the experiences of interaction.

You don't have to feel inadequate because your relationships are small compared to those of others.

Hold on to the certainty that if you're good like this, it means that you're good like this.

And if one day someone should ask you, stunned: how do you live with loneliness?

You answer that the moment you live together, you are not really alone: to live together you need two people!

Loneliness is not only poetry and contemplation but also introspection, the resolution of unsolved enigmas.

Loneliness is a method to go in search of the access code to your inner potential.

Do you want to unlock your inner potential? You must first take care of finding the unlock code.

And since what you want to unlock is your inner potential, you won't find the unlock code in the outer world.

Or you will. But it will only be a reflection of the code that you keep inside, and that you will project outside.

And then you won't see the code, but you'll see the projection.

You see, you have to be very careful about your inner projections that are reflected on the things of the world.

The mere projection of something is already a distortion of the thing itself. Every projected image can be distorted by light and shadow, by descents and ascents, by variations of shapes and colors on which it is projected, which gets confused with the image of the projection and generates a mixture that alters its original shapes and colors.

Remember: every projection is a corruption.

Every concretization of talent passes through a tortuous path of loneliness.

It is simply absurd to create, produce or plan while you are immersed in the chaos of society.

The chaos of society must be the inspiration, the events around you must be ideas in motion. Then, to track inspiration and ideas in motion, to channel them into your talent, you must leave the space of inspiration, and retreat into the space of creation.

The space of creation doesn't tolerate sounds, noises, voices, figures, images, smells, tastes, and shivers, because the creation requires absolute concentration, and absolute concentration is continuously interrupted by peaks of minimum concentration induced by perceptive, sound, visual, tactile, olfactory, taste distractions.

The space of creation is a sort of temporary arrest of the sensation.

You're the only one to be there, together with your memories and experiences. You're the only one to be there, together with your ability to process them. You're the only one to be there, together with your capability to transform them into art.

Be careful: when I talk about art, I'm not only referring to the common Arts.

Art is everything that—once immersed in the world—has the power to change people who encounter it, or simply the ones who make it.

Art is planning an adaptation strategy, art is planning a charity event, art is planning an escape from danger, or thinking about how to save someone from danger.

Art is the ability to take care of others. Altruism is art because it is the ability not to cede only to egoistic desires.

Do you want to unlock your inner potential?

Observe yourself and listen to yourself as much as you can, as deep as you can. But when you observe and listen, let go of all the visual and hearing interferences, all the images that make you feel humiliated, and all the chats that make you feel wrong.

Let go the vortex of past and possible future failures.

Pull negative memories and imagination out.

You don't need it.

There's only you and your infinite unexpressed potential.

Unexpressed, yes. But remember that the word unexpressed contains in itself the word expressed, which occupies much more space on the paper.

The expressed is infinitely more expressive than the unexpressed. And you can find it out. You only have to take care of erasing that initial un-.

I promise you will find the exact unlock code, and you'll find it pure, uncontaminated, unprojected—which means it won't reflect the things of the world—but entirely pure, precise, firm, compact behind you.

But how do I find this unlock code if everything good is obstructed by the rotten?

If you want to get rid of the mental rotten, free yourself from the rotten derived from interpretations.

There's nothing authentically rotten in your mind: what your mind identifies as rotten is the product of an interpretation.

Well, getting rid of the rotten means first reshaping the interpretation. Changing the sign and the drawing of the interpretation.

Are you able to redraw the edges of a drawing that has been there, under the dust for so long, that it seems the only possible drawing now?

Are you able to redraw the edges of a broken drawing, just to join the separation points?

If you redraw, for example, the interpretation of an impetuous fear that you felt in the past, you will see how, little by little, the obstruction that prevents you from accessing your inner potential will begin to become more and more phantasmatic until it disappears absolutely.

If you redraw, for example, the interpretation of a distressing failure that you have experienced in the past, the new lines of the drawing may take on the appearance of a door, and it will be the same door that will open wide before your inner potential.

It is an operation of overlapping, resizing, repairing, joining lines. Redrawing is a real redefinition.

Don't forget it, redefinition is always a step ahead of definition.

A definition is closed, it's a tightened room from which you don't think you can get out.

Redefinition instead is a way of fooling the definition, because the fact that you add something new to it, makes the room shapeable.

Try to make your mental rooms shapeable. I know you can do it. You know you can do it.

Remember the breath of abandonment that swept the overthinking's storm away?

Sometimes the breath consists of letting the mind go to its shaping and shapeable power. Accept to have a shapeable and shaping mind.

Your mind suffers. It suffers terribly when you try to wrap it into a fixed definition of events. The mind is—because of its nature—a flexible home, which rhythmically follows the restless motion of events.

Believe me, this isn't just a comforting story. A memory that tries to fix a painful event is a fake memory because it's not faithful to the inner dynamism of the event itself.

Chapter 3: Going Through Your Past to Improve Your Future

Let me tell you something.

Your childhood hasn't died.

The death of memory is possible only in the conscience, but what you bury in your conscience keeps on staying awake and living in the unconscious.

The archive of the mind is incredibly huge. And it seems like the unconscious doesn't know how to cancel the past because the unconscious is eternally present.

What lives in an eternal present move all the threads of memories, move memories like a puppeteer, or is moved by memories like a puppet, vibrates with words of a life lived, trembles with fears met who knows where, who knows when, who knows why.

It vibrates and trembles.

What is the difference between vibrating and shaking, if the movement is the same?

The difference lies in the feeling that is thrown into the movement.

The different content in the same form.

If you throw fear into the movement of the vibration, then vibrating becomes shaking.

You know, there are tremors that often seem inexplicable to us. Think about it: how many times have you found yourself shaking uncontrollably in front of a person, place, an object, a concept?

You were there, you were calm when your body suddenly started shaking as if it was a flag.

Here, you tell yourself that you can't tremble in front of something that has never scared us before. Yet you tremble. You tremble, and you don't know why.

In that space of doubt, in that nod of conscious uncertainty, your unconscious is actively operating. That unexpected tremor is proof that there is an underground agitation in you, of which your consciousness has no idea.

During your childhood, you've stored colorful fears that are now no longer remembered by your consciousness but are immediately present in your unconscious.

Well, it's better for your conscience to give up its role of the helpless spectator in front of the unconscious. In front of its power, even the most knowledgeable logic has to miserly step back.

But I don't want you to feel a slave of your unconscious. I want you to learn how to identify yourself with it, to domain it and to domain yourself.

Did you know that even your attitude of overloading with thoughts could date back to your infancy?

Imagine the scene. Your mom scolds you with an impulsive gesture, maybe while you're trying to catch a candy in secret, a forbidden candy, and she scolds you with these exact words: "You should have thought better of it!"

You were just a kid, so you repeated the mistake. And your mother scolded you, using the same exact words. And then again, and again. Until there was only one certainty in your mind: to prevent my mother's scolding, I should have thought better of it.

The problem is that repetitive inquiry of thinking better of it transformed with time into a waterfall of thoughts that appear before actions do. Only thinking is never a good idea: you have to think better of it. To sum it up, your mother wanted you to think better of it, and since she told you too many times, it assumed the form of overthinking.

Childhood is a tightrope between your family's voice and your inability to silence it.

You've never freed yourself from those voices. Still, you try to stay afloat in the same chatter that the child was flooded with.

And sometimes you still sink, and when you sink you feel like you can't breathe, and you tremble, tremble, tremble because it's the only way to move water and rise to the surface.

Shaking is a creative act of fear.

Fear creates its best choreographies with trembling.

You see, some dared to say that it's not possible to go back to change the past. They say the past must be accepted as it is. Oh, they told you a huge lie.

If it's true that the past lives in the unconscious like an eternal present, and if it's true that the present is in continuous change, it means that it's possible to change the past: it's sufficient to tune in to the unconscious.

Accessing the time of the unconscious means grasping past memories as if they were present moments. The past and the present intersect, coexist. And the present can be changed at any moment, as you wish.

To access the time of the unconscious it's necessary to hold back the discursive consciousness for a while.

The lower you bring the consciousness down, the higher the unconscious will rise, as in a balance.

Here is a small exercise that will facilitate accessing childhood memories. Remember that it must be repeated to work!

Sit in a completely darkened and silent room. Take a small object and move it rhythmically against an empty box.

Your brain must immerse itself completely in that repetitive noise, because the repetitive and insignificant noise, precisely because it is meaningless, turns off associations of ideas, and generates a condition of the emptiness of consciousness.

And it's exactly in the emptiness of consciousness that the presence of the unconscious is imposed.

After creating this condition of imaginative emptiness, after an attempt that must last at least half an hour, look for a song that you used to listen to as a child.

Put on your headphones. Listen to it about four times in a row until precise memories from your childhood emerge.

Try to drag those memories in front of you, catch them as if they were an insect buzzing in your ears. But beware of associations of ideas!

Repeat these words to yourself: I'm no longer in this present, I'm in the present of my childhood.

Enter the present of your childhood and change it. Try to hear your mother's voice as she reproaches you for an undisciplined action. Try to imagine her: "You should have thought about it better!"

Stop it. Block it. Pause the movie from your childhood.

Watch as your mother's lips open. Get in touch with your mother. Change the tone, change the words. Enter your mother's intention.

Go from "you should have thought about it better!" to "you have all the skills to guess the right behavior if you focus on what I tell you."

There's no longer the obligatory stage of thinking to improve pre-action, there's the stage of intuition and concentration.

And these are the exact elements that will allow you to achieve your goals.

Chapter 4: Stoic and Mindfulness Techniques to Leave Some Space for Useful Thoughts

Did you know you could live with absolutely useless thoughts?

Don't get me wrong, it's okay if a useless thought crosses your mind, from time to time. The problem is when a great number of useless thoughts start dominating—because of their intensity, impressiveness, and frequency—over the useful ones. When useless thoughts get inside the channels where your useful thoughts flow, they steal their place, time, and role.

You're probably asking yourself if this catastrophic scenario might actually happen. Look around. Or better, look inside of yourself.

It has already happened a thousand times.

But you didn't know. How could you, after all?

When useless thoughts make the useful ones fade away, something else happens as well: even the thought meant to reflect on the concept of "uselessness" disappears. Therefore, you weren't able to realize you were pervaded by useless thoughts. How could you have recognized them?

Useless thoughts are despotic and underhand: they conquer the forbidden space masquerading themselves as useful. The useless confuses itself with the useful, while it confuses you.

The useless abuses the fact that you don't really know what's useful to you, maybe because you've never thought about it deeply.

Have you ever thought about it?

Have you ever tried to classify what's useful?

Have you ever tried to look for the parameters to distinguish useful from useless?

Maybe you didn't wake up one morning, thinking "well, I'm going to select all the useful thoughts that cross my mind, and I will write them down."

Let's admit it, you've never done that. But I ensure you: it's not too late!

Take some time for yourself, to study yourself. Try to understand and find yourself.

The moment you find yourself, you will have found what's useful to you.

And when you got what's useful, you'll understand—by opposition—what's useless.

You have to claim to know what's important. Without knowing yourself, it's an intrinsic gamble: useful is subjective.

Therefore, useful thoughts are recognized, first of all, knowing the subject.

I want to propose a personalized exercise today, which takes inspiration from efficacious stoic principles.

The exercise is called: Illuminate your mental room.

Just like stoics, who identified themselves as people who could observe events from up above to get a clearer, detached perspective, you have to project yourself up above as well, and you have to identify yourself with the glass of the lights fixed on the ceiling.

Observe yourself from up above. You're doubled. And you know what the best part about it is? That you can be in two places at the same time. And yet, you can be in two places without feeling alienated from yourself: when you "go higher", remember you're just getting away from your primitive and unconscious ego.

When you're higher, you'll see how every time the consciousness of events reaches a certain grade of illumination, the lights of your mental room will light up. Your mental room will light up.

How is it possible to get an illuminated consciousness of events? You'll ask yourself: how do I light my mental room up?

Well, you could try the "inner contradiction" technique.

Every time you formulate a thought on someone, on a sequence of situations, on an idea, ideology, feeling, emotion, sensation, imagine, challenge yourself with contradictions.

Try to formulate a thought which contradicts the thought you've just formulated.

Then try to respond to the contradiction in kind, as if it was a flame on a social network.

Contradiction always leads to illumination, because it's the dialectic battle against divergent ideas, which ultimately leads to the ultimate truth.

Truth is always crossed by paradox. And sometimes, truth corresponds to the paradox itself.

Try to think about the corpuscular and undulatory nature of quantum particles: it was a real paradox for classical physics, yet that paradox is now a scientific truth.

So, can you imagine how many quantum scenarios there are in your mind? That is, can you imagine how many paradoxical truths exist in your mind, that you can't see because you're afraid of confronting yourself with the paradox?

You know, it's not easy to begin to intuit the truth of paradoxes, because the first reaction in front of the paradox is confusion, disorder, dizziness. You say: heck, I didn't expect that!

Because the paradox embodies the unexpected.

What's necessary now is a great act of courage to find the truth of the paradox.

The surprise-effect seems to be generated by mental disorder, which follows the breakup of a usual order.

What if the paradox, rather than being the breaking of an order, was the intervention of a larger order?

Well, after experimenting with these two techniques—Illuminate your mental room and Inner contradiction—as tools to know yourself better, let's see how some Mindfulness techniques could help us.

1) Pay Attention to the Rhythm of Your Breath

Nobody teaches us how to breathe, right? We're used to thinking that our breath succeeds at managing itself all alone and that it does it perfectly.

That's true. But not entirely.

On one hand, it's true that our nature programs us for perfect self-management; on the other hand, it's also true that our unconscious influences can interfere with the regular rhythm of breathing. And here we find ourselves breathing in an uncoordinated way without being aware of it. The only way to become aware of this is to concentrate on breathing.

Pay attention to how you breathe. Try to catch and isolate all the moments in which you'll feel it is unregulated and ask yourself:

What did I do today to disturb my unconscious? What did I avoid saying? What did I say? What did they tell me? What did I see? What did I hear? What did I eat?

And so on, until you get to the main behavioral variations that there had been that day.

This way you'll be able to trace back the origin of your source of stress.

2) Pay Attention to Your Posture

When your posture is incorrect, you could place some obstacles ahead of your natural energetic flow. Purifying energy needs to circulate in a linear way, without interruptions or tortuosity.

3) Control the Music That Controls You

How many times have you tried to concentrate on something, but you realize you were terribly invaded by the chorus of a song?

Music has a brutal power, because of the ability to enter our minds and memory, and because of the difficulty of getting rid of it.

Be careful! This power could be a serious problem for your creative and intellectual performance.

Since the chorus of a song is a circular repetition of the same thing, it doesn't add innovative elements able to enrich you. And it could even inhibit your reflections and considerations, which could find it hard to be articulated, fade away and mix up with the repetitive sound.

4)   Place a Hand Lens on the Present

It symbolically means that you should focus on your present. How many times have you really tried?

Maybe you never stopped to tell yourself: okay, I'm living my present right now.

I can shape something, in my present. I can re-orient my path in both space and time, in my present.

Maybe you've never stopped the flow of memories, which cyclically come back, grasp your present and obscure it.

Placing a hand lens on the present means becoming the moment you're living. Because what's happening right now is so big that it could hold you entirely.

And when you become the present, you become the time. And when you become the time, you decide the course of events: events are not outside of you, but they're subjected to you, events are under time's domain.

Chapter 5: How to Practice Mental Minimalism

The strongest desire for a human being doesn't lie on the fulfilment of that desire, but rather in the desire itself.

The desire is restlessness, dynamism, vital fullness. Its fulfilment is quiet, stasis, boredom. And it's not about "always wanting better," or "always wanting more." It's about wanting always. Because something perennially unfinished is something that perennially attracts us to itself. What's accomplished doesn't even give us the time to want it, because it's already with us. The finish line that marks the end of the race is only yearned for while running, after which, once stepped on, it remains only a beautiful memory.

Now, try to imagine.

Your mind is a skein of small, unfulfilled desires. From the most probable to the most improbable ones. Your mind spins around from a desire to another, slow or fast, brushing against your goals, sure that it can give you whatever you've always wanted.

And yet, something paradoxical happens. Fulfilment is replaced by emptiness.

Here we go again: truth is crossed by the paradox.

Any kind of accumulation, even the accumulation of satisfactions, victories, triumphs, applauses, produces immobility, because it doesn't push you towards the research of essential things: on the other hand, it confines you inside the track of egocentrism which it gratifies by its continuous retracement.

You see, the idealization of an artist is his condemn, since the idealizing concentration, which cyclically retraces the sterile thoughts of glory, steals time and way of creation.

His idealization becomes his denial.

It's better for anyone who aspires to the fertility of ideas and the vigilant ignition of creative genius, to stay away from exaltation.

In this case, minimalism can help us.

Minimalism is a way of thinking which helps remove everything that distracts people from the essence of things.

Before reaching the level of eliminating useless desires, it's important to practice the elimination of useless objects.

1) **Think about Two Objects That You Don't Use Anymore but That You've Never Thrown Away Because You Felt Somehow Affectionate**

Pick them up. Think about someone who could need them. Give them away. Get rid of two useless objects and you'll be also freed of the affective bond that prevents you from leaving them.

2) Don't Look for The Support of Other Minimalists. Don't Look for Approval, Don't Try to Enter Groups of People Who Practice Minimalism

Minimalism is first self-sufficiency and autonomy of thought: you don't need others' approval to get rid of things you don't need. Often, others' approval is just a knick-knack, just like those objects you're no longer using but still can't manage to throw away.

3) Remember: Collateral Events Are Just Temporary

When you empty a suitcase, and you feel melancholic because of the end of the trip, it is the same thing as when you start the minimalist path.

When you start emptying your mental suitcase, you might feel melancholic.

But don't be afraid! It means it's working! No trial of great transformation could avoid the painful phase.

The greatest the pain from the liberation, the grates the joy to fill the suitcase with something new.

4) Project Yourself in the Future of Filling

When you feel the emptiness looming, both outside and inside, don't give in to the temptation of torment!

Rather, project yourself into the future of filling. Repeat these words: every emptiness of today is the filling of tomorrow.

Visualize your radiant and full-of-utility tomorrow, which you are already building by eliminating the uselessness of the superfluous.

5) Did You Know That Self-Realization Can't Happen Without the Emotional Impulse Towards the Other?

Think about it: even the most egocentric of humans can't do without the Other. Any center, by definition, needs space around it.

Well, having ascertained that the Other is indispensable to the realization of the Self, you can use your new minimalist ethics to do good to the Other.

Remember that authentic good is not what you "reciprocate": authentic good isn't done to family members, but to needy strangers, because good to strangers is never returned-good, but is the generative-good.

6) Understand the Reasons Why You Are Hesitant to Get Rid of Certain Objects

When you're thinking about the objects to get rid of and you feel hesitant, go back to that moment, stabilize yourself in that moment. Ask yourself: why am I having difficulty letting go of this object? What does it really represent to me? What would happen to me if I got rid of it, without too much trouble?

Through a series of introspective questions, you will be able to investigate your psyche, and this can help you when you are a victim of toxic attachment. You will be able to access the ground of your attachment, to the roots of your emotional movement.

Well, now you have a complete overview of the minimalist lifestyle.

What are you waiting for? Start now!

You have a lot to prove to yourself.

Chapter 6: 10 Suggestions to Immediately Improve Your Life

Here you have a list of ten things you immediately must stop doing to improve your way of behaving and thinking:

1) **Stay Away from People Who Bother Your Mental Health**

Stay away from disharmony. It doesn't belong to you, it's not connatural to your way of feeling. Remember that every off note leads to the rebellion of intonation, which perfectly knows its worth, and it also knows that it can't be corrupted by the clash of a repeated mistake.

Stay away from people who guide you towards disharmony. You will never belong to them, they're not connatural to your way of feeling.

When you are with someone, and you feel a light turmoil, a strange restlessness, or fear… it doesn't matter if it's the person you love the most, please, try to run away. Not right away, obviously. Do some experiments. Try again. But don't force the grip too much: if the door doesn't open, if turmoil is still there, it's better if you just change the door.

2) Try to Reduce Sugars

I know it's not easy. I know. But how can you expect to achieve results that are difficult to achieve by others, if you don't set yourself difficult goals?

Let's try something. Do you want to feel special? Do you really want to be special?

Good. Do something that others can't do! If nobody around you seems to be able to reduce the quantity of sugar they consume, you can be different with a simple decrease of amount.

It's not a real sacrifice: rather, it's the conquer of a quality of which others lack.

3) Throw Your TV from Your Balcony (But Make Sure Nobody's Underneath!)

Do you really know how dangerous TV is?

Let's talk about words. Let's consider the language.

Well, we know that nowadays TV welcomes anyone. Everyone can talk, even the ones who can't.

Well, know that every time you turn on the TV, there's a risk that you will run into the wise judgments of someone who can't speak.

Do you think you can observe the phenomenon in a detached way?

Sorry, it doesn't work that way. Our brain goes about its business: if you repeatedly make it hear a badly contextualized word, sooner or later it will learn it and think it's true. And sooner or later it will start suggesting that you miss-contextualize that word.

TV is full of unreliable witnesses of words! Don't let your language be distorted negatively: the next unreliable witness could be you!

4) Become the Conductor of Relationships, Not the Chaser

It may not be a scientific law, but I assure you it could become one, one day: the more you chase someone, the more they will escape from you.

Human beings are irremediably attracted by the unreachable. And you can observe it even in children's behaviors, which testify the authenticity of human nature.

It's like when kids stick out of the cradle, which is full of colorful toys, to grab an ugly and broken one. The kids don't really want that toy: they desire the toy that others don't let them take.

And believe me, desiring the unreachable is not a juvenile behavior: on the contrary, it's the baby that—having no social influences or objections—manifests openly the universal desire of the unreachable.

This desire belongs to every one of us.

But we tend to repress its center because the continuous tension towards something that can't be reached could lead to a state of endless unsatisfaction.

In any case: stop chasing people, they'd get bored!

Be an unreachable toy for them, and you'll see they'll stick out for you, just for you.

5) Reduce Your Use of the Mobile Phone

Too many repetitive actions. Too many already-seen configurations. Too much endlessly retracted information in various forms: the most harmful ingredient of social networks is repetitiveness because it atrophies the thought. A thought forced to endlessly frame the same image, the same notifications, the same contents, has no more reason to create new connections.

Protect your thoughts from atrophy: avoid web repetitiveness.

6) Don't Compare Your Life to Others' Lives

Stop comparing your life to others' lives: you'll never get to achieve an impeccable, logical equality.

Any attempt to overlap your experiences with others' experiences is fallacious and disastrous.

If you see someone reaching something that looks like a huge goal, remember that to that person that goal may be an unbearable burden that prevents them to sleep, or maybe it's the engine of a dark responsibility: to feel that they're living up to that goal for the rest of their life.

There are infinite perspectives from which one can look at people's goals, but then tell me: why do you always choose the one that makes you feel less fortunate?

7) One Goal at a Time

Since concentration is a fundamental factor to reach a goal, it will be very easy to understand that having too many objectives at the same time generates a messy net of goals, which will automatically inhibit concentration. How can one concentrate if every center vaguely mixes with the other?

Focus on one goal at a time. Not a mixture of centers, but one center at a time, which will slowly incorporate all the other centers.

8) The Past Is Just a Lesson to Let Us Understand What Went Wrong

Maybe it's surprising, isn't it?

Maybe you'll be wondering: how can the past—full of images, voices, sensations, emotions—can be only a lesson to underline a mistake?

Okay, maybe it's not this compulsory. What I mean is that our memory has many tasks, from a neurophysiological point of view.

But from the mental-wellness perspective, well, it's possible that you're making it dysfunctional.

Memory has the specific task to remind us that touching a pot full of boiling water might hurt us, and then suggests to us to stop to prevent us from suffering.

But tell me: how often do you use your memories just because of their function of avoiding pain?

How often, instead, do you use memories to increase the pain because of nostalgia?

9) Reduce Social Networks and News, Because You Don't Need Them (If The End of the World's Coming, Someone Will Warn You!)

I'm serious, it's not necessary for you to live in the continuous chaos coming from current information.

There is just a few relevant news for an aware citizen: most of the news that you daily hear is just a different reformulation of the same secular contents.

Your reading key may change throughout the years, but it can't surely modify itself in half a day!

Take a pause. Let events flow.

Come back when you're feeling transformed, and you'll know how to interpret things differently.

10) Be Present and Follow Your Dreams, Instead of Focusing On Others' Dreams

Here's a truth: the more time you spend observing others' dreams, the more you'll lose sight of yours.

Chapter 7: Find Out How to Win Over Indecision

When nothing's going as you planned it, is it possible that the universe is preparing you for the beauty of the unexpected?

Too often we step back because we fear that a single step ahead could mark the end of hope and the beginning of failure. But is it true that a single step contemplates all this power?

Maybe not.

Maybe it's just the perspective from which we're observing the step.

What's a step ahead, compared to a path full of steps back?

The moment of parking, of bursting pause, which interposes between a step back and a step ahead, is called indecision.

Exteriorized indecision is nothing more than a step, half away between moving backwards or afterwards.

Where do you want to live?

Where do you want to talk?

Where do you want to think?

Do you really want to stay there, in that dull fog of indecision?

Or do you want to re-start firmed time?

You see, it's not about fixing a broken watch.

It's about building a brand-new watch, which won't tend to break anymore. An indestructible watch.

Your new indestructible watch will be a race.

A race that no longer stops to see if it's better to take a step forward to reach the finish line, or if it's better to take a step back to reset the course itself.

The race of your indestructible watch ignores any kind of step back and only knows how to step ahead.

Because it's structured to measure victory.

It can be built by destroying indecision.

Destroying indecision, time will have no more leaps. Your time will never be broken or split again.

Your life will be illuminated by a new regularity.

Do you want to know how to win indecision?

In this case, I will share an infallible secret with you.

Someone calls it: the rule of the 40%.

But maybe calling it a rule is not correct.

Actually, rather than a rule, it's just a way to overturn rules.

When your brain suggests you're overcoming the limit, you immediately have to think you're just at the 40% of your real capabilities.

I assure you that indecision, in reaching a certain goal, won't even have the time to show up: it will already be disconnected from your thought.

Keep in mind, though, that this rule-non-rule can't be applied to everything: if there's a physical attempt, it's important to follow the brain's suggestions, because in that case, your body is the one who's talking, not your mental insecurity.

On the contrary, when it comes to intellectual efforts, it's possible to dare for more.

We will never really know our intellective limits: there's not an accurate test to measure the maximum effort our brain can make.

Are you sure you want to stop now?

Are you sure that your intellectual strength runs out at this exact moment?
We don't know the dynamic oscillations of the exhaustion of intellectual force, because intellectual force, by definition, escapes us continuously.

Already in the mere attempt to try to grasp it, we had to use the same intellectual strength that we claim to study.

Maybe the limits that we have imposed to our brain are much more flexible than we imagine.

The rule of the 40% teaches us that we haven't even reached 40% of our real capabilities.

Let me repeat it to you: the limits we impose to our minds usually come from wrong learnings.

Maybe we've done some demanding activity during a stressful day, and we automatically associate the exhaustion we feel at the end of the day with some general exhaustion due to that activity.

But that exhaustion is not general, is specific.

If the attempt wasn't repeated on a calm day, maybe after a good night's sleep, full of peaceful sentiments, then that judgment on the exhaustion of mental strength is incorrect, incomplete.

When you'll have built your indestructible watch, no continuous winds of indecision will brush against your intentions.

Your life will get better, I promise.

When hesitation stops breathing and time breathes a new, linear air, without the classical interruptions due to hesitation, I can assure you that life will be more comfortable, and easier to live.

Your relationships will unburden because for every choice you have to make there's a certainty: you will decide.

And this is a huge role in relationships.

The ones who have the power to decide, in a relationship, have already won.

Furthermore, since we already have talked about numbers, don't forget about the principle of the 80/20.

20% of causes produce 80% of the effects.

What does that mean, in detail?

Well, just think about the incredible implications of this principle.

Imagine: one day you're angry at God, you decide to throw out the window the picture of a holy image. Just around the corner, there's a man sitting on a bench. He's crying his eyes out. Doctors just called him to tell him his wife is going to have complications during the childbirth. They tell him that only a miracle could save her. At some point, the man sees the figure you've thrown out the window. He picks it up.

There's writing on it: Don't stop hoping.

The man smiles. He thinks: It's a sign!

He gets in the car, runs to his wife, comforts her; he tells her the most reassuring words of the world.

And in the end, the miracle really happens.

The miracle is that the man hasn't stopped hoping.

His wife gets saved, who knows how and why.

But let's get back to you.

You've only made a gesture, gripped by anger. And that's your little cause.

The effect of your gesture had a huge impact, it's gone through a big hospital, and saved two desperate hearts, a family that was about to be destroyed.

Can you see the gap between your actions and what corresponds to your actions?

This can happen also with success. It's enough if you light a spark, and success will fly around you like that holy image did with the miracle man.

Chapter 8: Find Out How to Win Over Procrastination

How many times have you heard the word "Procrastination?"

Who knows how many time people threw it against you with a certain irritation, who knows how many times it appeared like a scolding, a judgment, a sharp edge, and who knows how many times you stuck it on yourself, all by yourself, as if it was a self-critic, or just because you thought it fitted you, and nothing seemed to describe you better than the word procrastination, which has such a harsh and fleeting sound.

It's fleeting because it's always beyond itself.

Procrastination evades continuously itself because it's a word that doesn't want to fulfil itself in the present. And this is why it goes away even from itself, and moves further and further, until it becomes a fading figure, imperceptible to its other half.

A spring that doesn't want to join the two extremes, so the second extreme rebels and escapes.

The meaning of procrastination postpones itself endlessly, in order not to be finished.

And maybe it waits for somebody to run after it, knowing that when it will be reached, it will be too late.

The procrastinator is nothing more than the projection of this movement.

But to escape a commitment, they must not run, they just need to stop.

The procrastinator is stopped. They are aware of being stationary. They know their objective; they know the risks of that stubborn postposition.

They swim in the waters of postponement and breathe underwater in order not to go outside, and even sink, so they don't have to go up again.

But why? Why does this happen?

Why does the procrastinator postpone what should be done in the present?

Why do they find the future so charming, and the present so hating?

Maybe it's important to focus on the procrastinated objective.

One should ask: do you really want what you're postponing?

Things one desires can't be postponed: hugging a beloved one after years of separation can't be procrastinated. You know that well. Then, maybe the deepest reason for procrastination relies on the deepest reason for the objective.

Motivation. How much is it? How much do you need?

You see, when you're tempted to procrastinate something, you have to call your reasoning to the rescue. The first thing you have to ask yourself is: am I really motivated to reach this objective?

Probably, it will seem like you have no answer. You'll answer well, I don't even know myself if I really want it.

The answer exists. It exists in your own hesitation.

A hesitating answer already is the manifestation of a defect: the defect of sureness.

And when you're not sure whether you like something or not, you probably don't like it.

Attention! This doesn't mean that procrastination is the right thing to do.

There's a big difference between Pleasure and Good.

Imagine getting sick of an illness that can only be cured with a fruit, a very rare fruit. Imagine that this fruit is the essence of disgust and will lead you to the opposite pole of Pleasure. But imagine that this fruit will save your life and will lead you towards the pole of Good.

If you don't find this rare fruit in twenty-four hours, you'll let yourself die.

At this point motivation plays a decisive role; it pushes us to reach for something unpleasant, but it leads straight to the Good.

People who really want to live will immediately get their head in the game and look for disgust if it's the only way to survive.

People who don't really want to live will probably delay the research. They will concentrate more on disgust than on the achievement of the Good.

Because that Good, to them, is not that... Good.

But twists and turns!

What if I told you that the procrastinator will regret his choice just a couple of minutes before dying?

What if I told you that the procrastinator will suddenly feel a great desire to survive, just when death is about to be inevitable?

What if I told you that the procrastinator will wish to get rid of that illness when they have no more time to heal?

The secret to stopping procrastination is understanding in time what's good for us and comprehending in time that pleasure isn't always identified with the good because pleasure could also lead us to the bad.

The relationship with food teaches us this. Every day.

Perhaps nature has tried to give us an indication when it has endowed with a bad taste the so-called foods that do well.

Yes, it is as if nature has put a warning label on it, which reads more or less these words: what seems to you an absence of pleasure can lead you to a greater good than its presence.

However, it remains to be understood how to... understand what Good is.

All right. Let's talk about dreams.

You have a dream.

And for you, Good corresponds to realizing that dream. Right?

However, the path from study to dream is full of obstacles and boring situations.

So, what happens? It simply happens that boring situations take over the target of your dream.

Maybe you forget about it. You forget about its importance. You lose yourself while studying, and you forget the reason why you're studying.

So, you start procrastinating boring activities, because you can't project your dream in the present. You can't project the future in the present. That's all. And that's the secret.

Projecting the future in the present re-increases the lost motivation!

Believe me. You'll find your motivation again.

You have to start by doing what I call: exercises of projection.

It's about empowering the desire of your dream, and therefore re-conquer the desire of the Good.

When you realize you're procrastinating, take everything away from you. Objects, food, people. Take them away. Take immediately a pause from the activity that distracts you, whatever it is. Use that pause to focus your thoughts only on your dreams.

Are you there?

Good. Now, travel with fantasy. Visualize your dream, almost realized, as if you were just a step away from it. Reconstruct the possible scenarios. Afterwards, build up a mirror in your imagination. Go look at yourself and take a picture of your thoughts: what you see, reflected on the mirror of your imagination, is the smile that enshrines your dream has come true.

Chapter 9: Ideal Zen Meditation That Will Make You a Better Person

Do you know that background light of thoughts that regularly accompanies you during the days and seems almost to proceed on its own, while consciously, you think you are focused on something else?

That's the discursive conscience.

One of the most fascinating things about the thought is that—differently from words—it foresees the overlapping of two or more voices in a single thinking subject: discursive conscience is a clear example.

Even when we're taking a break, we're subject to a continuous wander of the mind, and all of this could make us feel impotent, compared to its restless activity.

But that's where FA Meditation comes in.

What is FA Meditation?

It's a type of meditation based on the techniques of Focalization (F) and Attention (A). One of the fundamental elements of the meditative experiences is the exact capability to stop the discursive conscience and, consequently, check with awareness the DMN.

What's the DMN?

The DMN is a cerebral system that participates in the inner modalities of cognition, and it activates itself when someone is not focusing his attention on the external world, but rather on his interiority.

DMN is composed of multiple subsystems, among which we can find the temporal-lateral cortex, the angular gyrus and the hippocampus.

Furthermore, thanks to the almost mental emptiness produced by meditation, from the incessant repetition of a syllabus which has no meaning and therefore creates no mental image, for some instants our mind is free from the world's superstructures, from language, elaborations, classifications, measurements, arriving at a primordial state that can be easily defined phenomenologically: giving up thinking, one inevitably gets to the phenomenon of thinking, to the thought itself.

Hence, thanks to meditation, it's possible to send away that annoying discursive conscience and experiment a new, uncommon silence.

But how is it possible for meditation to make us more aware of ourselves? If it's true that meditation stops my thoughts, then it will also prevent me from thinking about my awareness!

Completely wrong.

Being aware doesn't mean thinking to be aware.

Awareness doesn't identify itself with the thought of awareness.

Awareness is a state of being independent from the thought: it's pre-verbal, pre-logical, pre-structured. It's a very big pre that includes a thousand post phenomena.

The thought is an after. It's never a before!

Awareness comes before anything else: because it pre-exists the existence of rational thought.

In the exact moment, you try to express this awareness through words, at the moment you articulate the awareness inside of a series of thoughts, and even during this attempt to tell you what awareness is, we're doing nothing but dancing around it.

In concrete, we never get to the purest core of awareness.

To get to its nucleus, well, one needs to move away from his ego.

Awareness is decentered.

The ego is egocentric.

And up to the moment, we feel the necessity to define ourselves with the tool of words, until we need to say, "I am" and "I think", we're still rooted into our Ego.

Meditation blocks the flow coming from the verbal thought, silencing words' notification. It sends away the conceptual thought.

And this is why it inhibits—even for just a few instants—the necessity to think "I am" and "I think".

Maybe we won't be un-rooted from our ego, but at least we'll get distracted from it for a little bit.

And that distance is sufficient to the center of our conscience to start looking at the center of awareness.

The Space of Action That You Subtract from Your Ego Will Be Filled from the Action of Awareness

Meditation is a precious practice.

You may find it boring in the beginning, but then—I assure you—it will be perfectly normal.

It's just the ego's superficial reaction. It's scared of withdrawal, and it addresses you towards feelings of boredom and irritation. It wants to stop you from your climb towards awareness. That's all.

You won't let its reaction to drag you too down, will you?

Don't be fooled by your own thoughts: it's not true that every thought that crosses your mind is authentically yours.

Your mind is crossed by a million thoughts that reproduce the personalities you've been and that you no longer are, which reproduce the personalities of people you met, and people you imagined meeting, and the idealized ones, censored ones.

To find the True movement in this chaotic movements of masks, to find the authentic thought in this flow of artificial thoughts, you need to get away from the ordinary state of conscience: the ordinary state of conscience is always contaminated by the ego's dominant position, and therefore subject to evaluation mistakes, logic turmoil, cognitive bias, etc.

One can light everything up with deep introspection, contemplation detached from the world, the objectivation of your feelings, the extraction of your thoughts, as if you were the witness of every thought you've thought about.

Becoming a witness of every thought, you will be able to recognize how many portions of these thoughts will actually be yours, viscerally felt, innate to you, and how many portions will be artificial, made up, built from schemes and hasty and erroneous elaborations.

And this is how we get to Zen Meditation, which was used by ancient men since it was able to provoke the reconnection to our real nature, with the pure and uncorrupted Being.

To practice it correctly, it's necessary that you improve your ability to focus on breathing.

You have to be able to let go consciously, deeply, without being distracted by interruptions, distractions, and interferences coming from sensorial or external stimuli.

Imagine being in your breath.

Imagine being your breath.

A breath that moves, stops, slows down, speeds up.

Imagine managing all the possible movements of your breath, which become your movements, when you identify with it.

Zen Meditation can alleviate stress, anxiety, negative thoughts, restlessness, sadness, and it can even regulate multiple bodily functions, such as sleep and digestion!

It's scientifically proved. Maybe you'll find many documents that strengthen this information.

Chapter 10: Guide to Improve Your Life in 21 Days

Workbook to acquire new mental and behavioral habits in 21 days!
- First week: self-knowledge.
- Second week: self-analysis.
- Third week: awareness.

Let's start with the first week.

Suppose today is Monday.

Let's take into account your skills and talents.

First of all: what is talent? And how many times have you told yourself that you have no talent?

Bergson wrote: "What's found in the effect was already in the cause."

Does it seem a trivial and simple phrase to you?

I confess that it seemed to me too, for some time.

Then something happened: I re-read it two, three times. And I began to hear a strange, gradual noise of footsteps in the alleys of my back thoughts. It was the sound of my thoughts saying: damn, even this new awareness, which is the effect of my stubborn re-reading, was already contained in the cause.

This sentence is simple, but it is of a simplicity that must first be crossed by complexity, in order to be accepted in all its fullness.

Simple -> complex -> return to the simple with the enrichment of the complex.

A dialectical procedure.

Bergson wrote that sentence with who knows how many different intentions, and somehow these intentions all exist, even if they are not unfolded, they are not disclosed in the effect.

Therefore, they exist in the cause (intention), but they do not exist in the effect.

Can it then be said that they all exist in a latent state?

I am convinced that we should all familiarize with the concept of latency, even in a transversal way, even with poetry, even with children's fairy tales. Who cares?

Well, maybe, when you think with conviction and resignation, "I have no talent" you will understand that maybe that talent exists, but it exists in a latent state, that is, it can exist occultly without manifesting itself in the effects (who knows, maybe because of the indisposition of external events that do not allow it to emerge to consciousness?).

You have no idea how big you are as a cause, and how small you are as an effect.

Try to regain confidence in the power of the cause, even when (who knows why) the effect is unmanifest.

Reacquiring confidence in the power of latent states: you will discover that talent is better at hiding than at not existing.

Good. Now it's time for some practice.

I ask you to make an effort of imagination.

Can you remember what it was like the first time someone said "*bravo*" to you and you, even for a moment, really believed it?

You were very small. I know. But right now, tell me: what were you thinking about?

There must be an activity that popped into your mind.

Drawing, painting, writing, music, matching, cooking, dancing, singing, acting, sports, translating, interpreting, playing, even a puzzle game, a word game, a number game.

Now you have read almost all of them. Here, can you tell me which word your eyes have been dwelling on for a long time? Can you tell me which word still echoes in your ears now?

Do you know that also interpreting a dream and succeeding at convincing the dreamer of your interpretation is a talent? It's the talent of the lawyer.

Even interpreting a dream and seeing the dreamer satisfied as if you just read his mind is a talent. It's the talent of the psychologist.

Also interpreting a dream and wandering with fantasy, adding fantastic elements that belong to your dreams is a talent. It's the talent of the poet.

Immersing yourself in someone's dream, feeling empathic for someone's nightmare, wanting to free them from his bad dreams, is a huge talent.

It's the talent of the ones who work with sick people. And they never get tired; to tell the truth, they never get tired of working, even when they think they're exhausted: comforting sick people is their passion, and every sign of exhaustion on their face is nothing but the sign of densified passion on their skin.

Please, now think about something you loved doing as a child, and that you had to abandon because of some external impediment.

Have you thought about it?

Well. Tell me if anyone ever told you that you were good at something and put it together with the activity you loved doing.

For example: if as a child you were told that you were good at drawing, and if as a child you loved to write, most likely your talent is in the artistic combination.

Writing and drawing have in common the combination of elements: a combination of syllables, words, phrases; the combination of shapes, colors, geometries.

Maybe your talent is halfway there: halfway between what you loved and let go, and what someone else loved about you.

The combination of these two eventualities could actually help you in the process of self-knowledge, which can't be said to be complete until you understand what your talent is.

Because yes, it's better if you resign: you were born with a talent!

And if you keep saying "I have no talent at all," you're actually showing great and rare talent.

Considering the number of possible talents that can dwell in us, don't you think that saying that you have no talent requires a talent already?

If you say so, it's because you have probably reviewed all the latencies of possible talents. Well, this is the talent of perseverance and sorting.

The first week of your transformation has to go through the phase of self-knowledge. It's essential!

Only by knowing yourself, you could re-know the solution to all your problems.

In the week of self-knowledge, I suggest you get isolated from the rest of the world.

It must be a period of inner recollection.

And to collect every memory and experience, it's necessary for you not to be

interrupted by new memories and experiences.

This is why it's important to pause.

It's fine if you just take a break from society.

Do you know that just a single week of total isolation could give you more illuminations than a year immersed in society?

Not bad as a balance, don't you think?

Is it worth it? Yes, it is.

You're not sacrificing anything: you're just rearranging your priorities.

And your priority is knowing yourself, knowing how to lead your life.

In the path of self-knowledge, after guessing what your talent is and what physical activity you're keen on, after having understood if your talent coincides with the activity you like, it remains to know the differences between happiness and contentment, to question what makes you really happy and what you believe makes you happy; what makes you really happy and what you believe makes you happy.

Contentment is not the same thing as happiness.

Did you know that?

When you said, "I'm happy," were you aware that maybe you were just content?

When you said "I'm content," were you aware of the fact that you might have been experimenting with pure happiness?

In your path of self-awareness and -knowledge, don't let your emotions get confused.

Known things must be clear, to achieve clear self-awareness.

Contentment is a word that recalls the meaning of containing: being content means to be contained in certain limits of satisfaction, without amplifying the lust for desire.

This feeling is certainly positive, even if it's not happiness, because we know that when the lust for desire expands limitlessly it leads to total dissatisfaction. After all, a desire without boundaries is not possible to be satisfied: where can one find, in fact, the satisfaction of something which is not specifically confinable?

Focus on your memories, now.

Tell me: what was the last time you've felt content? I mean, what was the last time you were really satisfied with a desire, without wanting to expand its intensity?

When did you contain lust without feeling it as repression?

Well, if you manage to pick some memories out of the archives, probably that memory will pop up spontaneously, without too much reflection, and it will be the truest one.

Let's move on to happiness.

How many times have you heard about happiness?

Looking for happiness, waiting for happiness, dreaming about happiness.

Happiness is declinable in every position and in any perspective because it's a universal feeling.

And as long as there is some human presence on this planet, anyone, anywhere, will be dreaming about pursuing happiness.

But what is happiness?

Not every search engine of etymologies agrees on the order of importance of its meaning, and yet there are some common elements to every one of them.

It's like when many doctors describe a disease that is the same in every place and time, but each of them emphasizes a different symptom.

The order of importance of meanings changes, but not the quality of meanings themselves.

An essential meaning of the word happiness starts from its root: abundance, wealth, prosperity.

But be careful not to confuse wealth with an obsession for money, abundance with the tension of accumulation, and prosperity with purely economic wellness.

Words are daughters of time, remember that.

And in the historical moment which sees the formation of the word happiness, wealth, abundance, and prosperity were not the same we refer to, today.

Is this why happiness keeps on escaping us all the time?

Perhaps it's because we don't know its original meaning. After all, we were born during the age of distortion of meaning.

Who knows how many senses we lost, because these senses went lost during historical transmigration from era to era, from voice to voice, from distortion to distortion, from flattering to flattering.

Original words were full of meanings, which gradually flattered throughout different ages.

And here we are, dealing with happiness without knowing what the first man who said, "I'm happy!" was thinking about.

Have you ever thought about it? Why did the first man on earth feel happy?

And now I ask you to do another mental experiment.

Re-read the above-mentioned question, and tell me if an image, a word, a figure crossed your mind. Whatever it is, I suggest you fix it for a little bit in your current thoughts.

Don't let it slip away.

Try to write on a sheet of paper everything that crossed your mind while reading the definition of contentment and then the definition of happiness.

It won't do much good now, but you'll have to pick up this note in the second week, in the week of the self-analysis.

As in any serious research, after collecting data, all that remains is to analyze it. And now you are the researcher, the meter and the guinea pig of yourself.

There's no one who can study you better than you can study yourself.

There's no one who can show you the way better than you can figure it out for yourself.

Me neither. My words here are as the springboard for your intuitions.

My Words Are Not Here to Tell You Who You Are, But to Remind You Who You Are

Don't trust people who want to tell you who you are: they're lying to themselves and to you as well.

Words are evocative forms. They're not truth-containers.

Hence, now that you had the chance to remember your talents, the activities you loved, and moments that made you feel both content and happy, do you know why you managed to remember them?

Because they already existed in you!

If you didn't already possess all the truth inside of you, my words wouldn't be enough to evoke them, because they can't evoke a non-existent content.

So now, get ready for a new challenge: egoism and altruism!

Have you ever thought about the difference between egoism and altruism?

Where do egoism end and altruism begin?

And if altruism makes me feel good, am I selfish if I want to keep on being an altruist to feel good?

Maybe the difference doesn't lie between altruism and egoism; they're intersected because in them coexist only a great feeling: The Good.

Perhaps the real difference lies in the space separating healthy selfishness from unhealthy selfishness. The selfishness that helps you, and selfishness that damages you. Egoism that protects you, and egoism that tears you apart. The selfishness that saves you, and selfishness that destroys you.

Maybe even altruism is a form of selfishness. But it's of the same substance as healthy selfishness: it helps you, protects you, saves you.

No altruistic act is ignored by the universe.

And since the universe is the conjunction of all separations, and since there is no distance in the universe between Me and the Other, being an altruist is the best way to catch its attention.

In the path of self-knowledge, you need to distinguish love from infatuation.

Thrills, palpitation, restlessness, strong desiring tension, exaltation, immediate madness, continuous ups and downs, sudden surges of sensations towards the same person: this is a synthesis of infatuation.

But what about love?

Perhaps everything that can be said about love has already been said by music, art, literature.

And you know what the result is?

The result is that after all the millenary representations of love, we have no idea what love is in its universal sense.

Each representation of love has only given us an idea of the particular love, but there is no trace, at least apparently, of universality: the concept of love can differ so much from a person to another that, in the end, it's legitimate to wonder whether universal love isn't, in fact, the sum of all possible conceptions of particular love.

So, being very careful not to fall into schematism that claims to universalize a single concept of love, I ask you: how did you feel when you felt love?

Remember that the definition is yours alone.

You can take any gamble.

You can even say that you've fallen more in love with your yard map than with a human being.

You can even say that you fell in love only when you were not reciprocated.

I will understand you.

I will understand, because love in itself is indefinable, and when we face something indefinable, we can certainly not be surprised to see something unsuspected.

Could infatuation be better than love?

I mean, that vortex of emotions typical of infatuation makes you feel alive more than ever.

And love? Love, if it's already accomplished, if it's never suspended, elusive, chased, what does it move? Does it move weaker emotions than infatuation?

It's possible.

Paradoxically, it's possible that infatuation is emotionally more powerful than love.

Or rather, it's possible that the concentration of a multitude of different emotions is more compacted in a few moments of immediacy, rather than deferred in many moments apart.

So, let me make a small observation on the danger of infatuation, on what negative impact can it have on your dreams, your ambitions, and your performance in general.

Since infatuation generates a vortex of strong emotions, it creates a recursive focus of the desired object, and it risks paralyzing any other idea.

In short: infatuation could suppress your creativity.

Fixed thinking is not only the wonder of desire but also the dark side of not being able to concentrate on an important task.

Sometimes, when you feel sick while you're infatuated, when you feel physical symptoms, try to ask yourself: what if it's the unconscious that rebels?

There is no worse suffering for the unconscious than unexpressed creativity.

It's not a coincidence that the most creative people fall ill with a psychosomatic disorder and their symptoms resemble a brilliant dysfunctional dance choreography of the body.

Even in the dysfunction, the creative genius emerges.

The unconscious can have fun creating even the dysfunction as long as it creates something.

And infatuation can be detestable to a creative unconscious.

You can't get out of the boundaries of infatuation: you only dance around the object of your emotional tension.

Infatuation is pure movement, but it forces you to move only within itself.

Infatuation is both movement and paralysis. And who knows if its bivalent magnetism makes it even blinder than love.

Is infatuation Bad? No, absolutely not.

In fact, one should experiment it, welcome it, live it.

Emotions shape, mark, and build personality. The emotional vortex of infatuation can't and shouldn't be avoided.

But...

Could your performance be negatively influenced by infatuation?

Yes, certainly.

For this reason, it's important to find a balance. When you have to do something important for your life, leave infatuation aside.

You may be thinking this is crazy. But how can be infatuation delayed, if infatuation is defined as such because of its uncontrollability?

Watch out. Be careful here. Because the essence of success lies all here:

The Ability to Control Accidental Events That Claim to Control Us

It's like when the chorus of a summer hit gets in your brain and you resign and say: there's no way to send it away, it's stronger than I am!

No, it's not.

The sound is strong, but not stronger than you.

If someone tells you that you can't control an event, don't believe them!

Do experiments. Experiment even with emotions and feelings. Yes, do exactly what no one would ever expect!

Isn't that what winners do, after all?

If someone tells them that they will fail, the winner doesn't believe them.

The winner literally challenged the odds and statistics, forecasts and conclusions of others.

And do you know why? Because those statistics, those forecasts, those conclusions weren't decided by them.

The winner doesn't leave others to decide, they decide.

Then you can experiment with anything, even emotions.

If an emotion gets in your way, believe me, it's not a law that you should let yourself be overwhelmed by it.

And it's not necessarily true that you will suffer from symptoms of repression: perhaps you will feel some malaise, of course, but if your purpose is good, if you have subordinated pleasure to do good, I guarantee that the malaise will last very little, and soon you will be able to observe the effects of Good in the short and long term.

Often overwhelming emotions are waves of coincidences that arrive to put us in front of a challenge: have you ever noticed it?

How many times does an infatuation pop up just when you're focused on an important project?

It's like the universe wanted to test your motivation.

And this is how we go back to the discourse of procrastination.

If procrastinating means having a weak motivation or forgetting how powerful motivation is, the fact of cheating, the effort to push away, to push the infatuation away, can undoubtedly increase the strength of motivation.

Being it an effort, it magnifies the strength.

And what is reinforced is precisely the motivation to achieve a certain goal.

Good. I would say that we're now entering a path one step higher than self-knowledge, to be more precise we're heading towards the path of self-analysis. The second week will have to be conducted under the banner of self-analysis.

What is self-analysis?

Nothing more than the summary of self-knowledge, from an analytical perspective.

The point now is not only knowing what we like doing and what our talent is, what's love and what's infatuation, but analyzing our inclinations and our preferences.

Why do you prefer love to infatuation? Why do you prefer infatuation to love?

The path of awareness, which is the extreme synthesis, must be walked with knowledge and analysis.

To start the journey towards self-analysis, I want to propose to you an experiment with words.

Bright.

Dark.

Eternal.

Temporary.

Can you tell which of these adjectives you use the most in your daily speeches?

Which of these adjectives escape you almost involuntarily? Which ones do you tend to apply to everything, as if they were a thought fixed in your unconscious and, if necessary, emerge in your conscience?

Remember every word that you frequently pronounce, every word that's scattered into your speeches, tells something about you.

Don't be indifferent to your daily language, because your speech communicates your way of being.

The first tool of self-analysis is paying more attention to trivial details.

Pronouncing a word is a process we don't pay attention to, we probably don't even recognize it, because we always have it at hand.

And it's universally known that everything we have at hand gradually becomes invisible.

The truth is, however, the unconscious choice of words to say underlies very complex mechanisms related to the structure of our emotional and cognitive systems.

For example, if the adjective you have chosen is Dark, I ask you to question yourself about the feeling that this word gives you when it's isolated.

That is, you don't have to apply it to any name. Just try to isolate it in your mind. Leave it free to drive out all its expressive power.

Describe to me the colors, shapes, shadows of this expressive power.

What makes you feel the word Dark?

Anxiety, sadness, turmoil, loneliness, alienation?

Or paradoxically... charm and enchantment?

You see, it's not that darkness has to necessarily indicate a negative meaning.

Darkness is the sleep of light, and light needs to sleep to recharge its light energy better.

Thus, loving darkness could mean that you love the energy source of light.

Do you realize how important it is to analyze the choices of our words?

We have this bad habit of analyzing just the words other people say. We don't do anything but ask ourselves things like "oh my God, why did he call me pretty but not beautiful?" or "why did he say he cares about me but not that he loves me?"

And yet, how can we analyze others' words if we don't clarify to ourselves the limits of our language?

Self-analysis is a starting point to the analysis of the Other.

The more you'll refine your self-analysis, the more you'll refine your analysis of the world.

It's about a continuous exchange between you and the world.

Self-analysis means understanding why we're feeling something when we're feeling something.

Tell me: what was the last time you cried?

I mean a serious cry, a cry people could hear, could hear explode. A cry you couldn't stop.

For whom, for what, did you cry?

You know that well.

But whoever it is, or whatever the reason for your last tears, must be analyzed.

You have to understand what damn power it has over your tears. Who gave it this power? Did you give it to it, or did it conquer it himself?

Have you ever felt deeply calm after crying?

Have you ever listened to a song, aware that that song would drive the engine of your tears?

I mean, you knew that and still looked for it anyway, you played it anyway. What did you want? Did you want to hurt yourself?

Many interpret crying as something tragic. And the will to cry as a self-damaging will.

You know, I believe that crying is the desire to find the lost order.

I imagine the imploded tears like messy water we have inside. And I imagine the tears exploded as a way to throw out of us that messy water, and therefore to let the disorder flow away.

And now, you can tell me.

Maybe you are looking for the song that makes you cry because deep down you like to cry listening to a forbidden song.

And do you know why you like crying while listening to a song? Because at that moment you can be a powerful human being: memory, feelings, re-enactment, imagination, fantasy, associations, melancholy, physical reactions, loss of control. You're actually sad when you stop crying.

Its beginning and its end are emotional oscillations because in its beginning there's the formation of the first tear; and in its end, there's its disappearance. Appearance and disappearance.

Crying is a rite of passage. To the emotion, its beginning and its ending are enough.

The logic of crying is extremely flexible.

And after all, self-analysis is also discovering your logic of crying.

I know that this path seems torturous and full of pitfalls. I know that the upheaval of the ideas that have made you up by others, and that you have accepted without question, is not comfortable. On the contrary, it's uncomfortable. Because it makes you flutter from one idea to another like a balloon that loses its air, and that air is made up of all the certainties that others have put into ideas. You need to lose your worn-out air. You need to lose your certainties, to move in the renewed air.

So, what are you waiting for? Rise up like that balloon. Untie the knot. Let out the old air.

Don't be afraid of collapsing on the ground like a deflated balloon.

You're not your form.

Do you know what else self-analysis is?

It's the analysis of how your healing works. They generally tell us that an annoying or painful symptom is a warning signal that something's wrong with our bodies. But that's not always true.

Other times, something painful or annoying tells us that healing's taking place. And paradoxically, the more intense the malaise of the symptom, the more effective the healing will be. It's like healing was for the body as painful as the disease itself.

Maybe the quantity of energy used is the same both to heal and to get sick.

Do you know what happens to your body when you have a fever? Well, one can say that fever is a sophisticated process of spontaneous self-repair. If your body is capable of rising fever, be sure that your body is intelligent, because it means it recognizes the threat and gets ready to eliminate it.

Trust your body. Treat it with love. Don't ever doubt its intuition.

If the philosophical theory of panpsychism was true, that is, everything in the universe is conscious, then there is the possibility that your body feels you, when you speak and think badly of it.

Let's say that all your organs are endowed with a rudimentary consciousness, similar to that of a human being in early childhood development.

Do you know what happens to a child when he's constantly criticized for not being able to do something?

It happens that the child becomes demotivated, closes in on himself, gives up, gets lazy, stops training to do better.

Now imagine that your heart gets demotivated, closes in on itself, gives up, gets lazy, stops training to do better.

What would you get? Certainly, not a heart working properly.

Therefore, in the doubt that panpsychism is a reasonable vision of reality, I propose you not to risk and treat your body better, as if it was a sentient being.

After all, what does it cost you?

Maybe the first time, when you try to speak with it, you could feel humiliated or deluded, because every time you don't pick up the response signals, and you feel like you're talking to yourself.

But I want to ask you something: if you were next to a comatose man, would you stop talking just because he can't give you any response signals?

Would you feel humiliated or deluded?

I ask you not to underestimate the possible omnipresence of consciousness.

You know, there are scientists who have even ventured the hypothesis that consciousness preexists in the universe.

That is a huge consciousness that exists before the big bang, since before the birth of the universe.

And then, seen from this perspective, maybe it's not that absurd to believe that consciousness allows all visible and invisible things in the universe.

Self-analysis also means: how many times have you consciously mistreated your body?

How many times have you not listened to it enough?

How many times have you continued to give in to vice, even knowing that this vice would hurt your body?

Imagine a dad filling his baby with toxic candies, even though he knows that the candies will poison him.

How Many Times Have You Not Been a Caring Father to Your Body?

You know, they say that when a child grows up unregulated, aggressive, violent, the blame lies primarily in the upbringing his parents gave him. And if no trace of it is found, then it'll be moved on to other environmental, socio-cultural, genetic factors.

Tell me: how did you educate your body until today? Has your body grown unregulated?

Don't blame yourself for anything.

If nobody ever told you, or if you have never thought it possible that your body could be sensible to your mood and education, it's not your fault!

You have nothing to reproach yourself: you're just the victim of information that hasn't reached you in due time. Or maybe, a victim of your awareness, which wasn't ready to accept certain suggestions (we are never guilty of an unprepared awareness, we're simply unprepared, that's all!)

The good news is that you're still on time to become everything you would like to become for a child.

Balance can be restored in any phase of the imbalance, even during the most disastrous phase.

And do you know why?

Because balance is the other side of the coin of imbalance. And when the imbalance is powerful, it will only be necessary to put more power into overturning the medal on the side of the balance.

Self-analysis also means asking ourselves how powerfully we are willing to turn the medal.

And above all, from where to collect the energy that will help us to overturn the medal?

Perhaps meditation can give you what you are looking for.

If it's true that in certain states of deep meditation we reconnect to the divine source, and if it's true that the divine source is pure energy, and if it is true that the divine contains everything and the opposite of everything, then it's in the baggage of the divine that the power of the energy devoted to overturning the medal must be sought, when stubbornly established on the side of imbalance.

All the words in the world can't compete with the very first core of meaning. Because in the very first core of meaning there are the seeds of all possible meanings from which all possible words will arise.

When you're meditating you exceed the speed of sound of words because you access the pure meaning.

And it's in its purest meaning, where all possible meaning resides, that the solution to imbalance lies.

The Source of All the Possible Meanings Is Also the Source of All Possible Solutions

Your path of self-analysis has to go through the verbal language, even just to arrive to the preverbal language.

Someone could dare say that it's a step back, the passage from verbal to preverbal language. Well, I say it's a leap in the abyss.

And the abyss is neither forward nor backward: it simply is.

This is how the passage from the word to its meaning is a wonderful leap into pure being.

Self-analysis is studying one's own body.

No. I'm not saying you have to become a doctor.

I'm saying you should study everything that scares you. And if what scares you is a certain part of your physical body, if what scares you is a certain organ of your physical body, then all you have to do is study what terrifies you, study its physiology, that is, to understand if it's right that you should be afraid of it, or if it's it who will start being afraid of your fear.

Do not underestimate the fear of the child. It can be more powerful than the fear of the adult.

You are the adult; the consciousness of your organs is the child you have to take care of.

But remember, we're talking about consciousness, not functioning. Don't fall into the trap that the functioning of your organs is rudimentary, just as rudimentary as their consciousness.

The Functioning of Your Organs Comes from Absolute Perfection

It's only the weight of time, environment, genetic alteration, that compromises that perfection.

While you're struggling to find the solution to your sore throat, know that your body already knows the biological remedy. It simply doesn't tell you and doesn't put it into action!

And if it doesn't, it's because that sore throat is itself functional to the holistic perfection of your body.

You know, self-analysis is also understanding what is functional and what is dysfunctional.

Self-analysis is realizing one's own limits of interpretation.

Because yes, we humans are full of cognitive limits that translate into interpretative limits.

Come on, how can you trust a perception that it's deceived by an illusory image?

Think of those illustrations on Facebook, the ones with the still images that our brain perceives as moving images.

The truth of that illustration is on the opposite side of our perception!

In short, we are in falsehood without knowing it.

And if nobody told us that that image was actually still, we would have kept on seeing images thinking to have met a moving one.

Do you get the cognitive gap?

Do you get that there could be a million other illusory things that crossed your mind and you thought them to be real?

We're so irremediably deceived by our perception, that before saying "that's true!" and "that's false!" we should ask ourselves if we really know the nature of truth and the nature of false.

Who taught us the nature of truth?

And who can assure us that the scholar of the real truth has actually understood what they have studied?

Self-Analysis Means Freeing Oneself from Others' Interpretations

On one hand, it's important to recognize the authoritativeness of the scholar of a certain truth; on the other hand, though, it's important not to conform one's interpretation with the interpretation of an authoritative person.

We must recognize the inestimable value of the scientific method, but we must not forget that there is a discipline, epistemology, which deals exactly with defining the limits of scientific knowledge. That is, the limits of our cognitive capabilities in the systematic study of the world surrounding us.

And if there are limits to what is considered to be the most reliable thing among all others (scientific knowledge), get ready to sink into an ocean of perceptive limits which will accompany our days!

The moment you'll analyze yourself, you'll have to come to terms with the fallibility of all the things you've stored under the name of certainties.

You will have to recognize and accept the fallibility of your certainties.

Because, you know, questioning is a fundamental step in achieving awareness.

What is it to be aware if not to be aware of one's own limits?

One can't aspire to become self-aware without first having eradicated the word "certainty" from an imperfect system of knowledge.

As long as we depend on this huge trap called perception, we should be cautious in recognizing the truth.

And you'll see that this way, the border between real and imaginary will become paler, thinner, crumblier.

We have always been told not to confuse reality with imagination, and we often read that ancient people did it because they were naive.

Actually, they're the same ancients who have had insights on which we have relied, and that today have allowed us to build the tools to be able to say, "it's a dream!" or "it's not a dream!"

Perhaps these ancients were not so naive... Weren't they?

Let's think of Pythagoras. Philosopher, mathematician, thaumaturge, scientist, shaman, politician, astronomer. Well, don't be too enthusiastic. If someone had to read his biography... he wouldn't find it hard to think of him in that faded naivety to which all of the ancients throw themselves, as if they were in a slop.

But would they have any idea of what a legacy of knowledge this "naive" Pythagoras has left us?

So, I say: if confusing dreams and reality also mean being so lucid to produce rational and rationally applicable knowledge in reality, which lasts for millennia, perhaps the interference of the imaginary world is not bad.

Be cautious in your judgments. Not only towards others but especially towards yourself!

Is it true then? People keep on making mistakes when attaching labels to other people; imagine what they do to themselves!

How many times have you attached to yourself the wrong label? Maybe, while you were conditioned by others' opinions, or maybe because you were eager to place yourself into a category, in a peer group, in a bubble of consciences similar to yours.

Without really understanding how much you had to share with that group, and how much you forced yourself to be, just to look totally alike to the members of that group.

You have distorted yourself so many times in the course of your life that, today, in order to rediscover your true nature, your pure, authentic, uncorrupted nature, you will have to retrace all the stages of your existence.

Yes, going back to authenticity involves a great effort of memory, concentration and, above all, detachment from previous knowledge. Detached from the impressions of others.

Get closer to your impression, find the expression of your nature.

If you have come this far without being in the least disturbed by my words, I want to tell you that the memories of every alleged truth are within you.

If you have come all the way here with a certain sadness about my words, I want to tell you that perhaps you have learned and understood more than you imagine.

The week dedicated to self-analysis ends with an examination of conscience. One does not enter the Path of consciousness without being in harmony with the Other.

Keep in mind: our cells are biologically programmed to cooperate, not to compete. So, if you are competing with your peers instead of cooperating, know that you're acting against nature.

Answer these questions:

1) How lenient were you with your neighbor? Have you refrained from judging them or have you given in to the temptation to comment negatively?

2) Make a balance of the positive and negative thoughts you had on the people around you. On which side of the scale does the needle hang?

3) What inspired your actions, thoughts, behaviors? Love or egoism?

4) Have you tried to be helpful to people in need?

5) Were your words and reactions in front of others guided by honesty or have you chosen to be dishonest not to make a bad impression?

6) Have you undergone an ego-tear from a lack of recognition by others? If yes, did you do that particular thing just to get recognized?

7) How much humility and how much arrogance determined your words?

8) Were you able to identify with other's pains and soothe the wounds? How much have you been able to identify with their pain?

9) Have you been more tolerant or more intolerant? More patient or more impatient?

10) How much did you manage to donate to others without expecting to be praised?

11) Have you allowed anger and envy to poison your feelings?

12) Did you try to disharmonize where there was harmony, or to harmonize where there was disharmony?

13) Did you help to make your social environment peaceful?

14) How much did you try to get rid of your fears?

Okay, now tell me. How do you feel?

Wait. Stop. Don't answer.

I know you're probably thinking you're inadequate, that you haven't met your own expectations, that you've found yourself blurred in the face of your insecurities, your weaknesses, your shortcomings. Maybe you weren't even thinking that there were so many incongruences with what is defined as cooperation, peace, harmony.

Let me tell you it's not what you think. It's not because of a lack of yours.

Maybe nobody cared to explain and remind you, and I underline *remind* you because anyone has the need to remember the importance of good feelings at regular intervals—all that one has to apply to break down competition and favor cooperation.

Stay calm, even if you haven't passed this examination of conscience. Do you bet that, after remembering all the good rules, you'll pass it brilliantly next time?

It's like studying for an exam.

Reading is not enough; repetition is needed to imprint a concept in the memory. In the same way, maybe it's necessary to repeat even painful experiences, to imprint in our memory that the Bad is not the right choice.

When there's no pain, remembering the Good is difficult.

Because, as it happens in many other things in life, one remembers by opposition.

We perfectly know how to turn the light on. But we have learned to do it to face darkness. It's during dark times that one remembers how to turn the light on.

In the bad, you remember the good to do. In the good, we remember the bad to avoid.

Two forces that coexist in their formal incompatibility.

The path of awareness is already beginning to open up for you, as soon as you realize the inseparable relationship between good and evil, and the mutual influence that makes them as they are to themselves.

Good is identical to itself by virtue of the difference with something else from itself: Bad. And vice versa.

And yet, you realize that this identity and this difference are so feeble when you move backwards, and upwards, and still upwards, and you see from an absolute perspective what has always been under the gaze of the Absolute.

Have you ever tried to identify with God?

They told you that it's impossible, yet we can't help but identify ourselves even with what seems impossible to us to embody.

So many of us said "if I had been God, I wouldn't have created...I wouldn't have done...I wouldn't have moved... I wouldn't have... I wouldn't be..."

Yes. At the limit of human exasperation, a man says: I would not be. He prefers nothingness to being. He identifies himself with God and says: I would have done nothing; I would have been nothing.

There are many people who aspire to nothing.

And yet there are too many people who are suffering to death and have no intention of dying!

What happens there, among those people? What makes pain so bearable, when pain is the only way to stay alive?

Is life tolerable even at the end of pain?

If this is so, Good has already won Evil. For even in the most atrocious Evil, there is at least one reason to see the presence of Good. And this reason is contained in life. Or at least… in the life of those who want to keep themselves alive.

I'm sure that the path of your awareness is already paved. Even more so, if only once, in reading these words, you said: hell, that's exactly what I thought!

Pure intuition is always one step ahead of language. The author of this book is a linguistic channel of your deepest insights.

Don't forget you already contain, in the form of pure intuition, all the information you read in the form of linguistic signs.

Your consciousness doesn't contain them, because it's incomplete by definition. Your unconscious does. Your unconscious, as a source of omniscience, contains all possible information.

Awareness arises—first of all—with a detached summary of past events. How can we summarize these pages? We've evaluated the risks and dangers that hide behind overthinking.

We have also revealed the damages that overthinking causes both to ourselves and to other people.

We have pacifically agreed that you're a brilliant person even if nobody tells you that, because your brilliance makes people who look at you speechless. We've observed that the most intelligent people are the selective ones, who are so focused on their goals that they don't even realize when a more consistent relationship's missing.

We have elaborated techniques to unblock your mental potential, a potential that doesn't stop existing, not even when it's sleeping.

We have found out that your way of thinking is inextricably linked to your childhood, and therefore it's not improbable to think that overthinking is the consequence of wrong teachings.

We have also stated that going through the past can change both the present and the future if while going through it, the events are correctly re-interpreted.

We have chosen to send away all the useless thoughts to reach your goals and increase the space for useful ones. And to do that, we approached Stoic and Mindfulness techniques.

We have gone through several steps to effectively tidy up the chaos that dwells in your head, relying in a particular way on the minimalist ideal.

We have drawn up a list of ten things that you must stop doing to improve your way of behaving and your way of thinking. (And who knows if you have already started to stop?). Have you taken people who threaten your psychophysical health away from you? Or rather, have you identified them? Before driving them away, you must identify them, recognize them. Have you committed yourself to this operation of discernment? Have you tested the changes in your mood according to the people you encounter?

Well, if you have done something like this (or even thought about doing it) I can tell you that you have understood the goals of this manual.

And who understands, sooner or later takes.

You'll take everything you are entitled to from reality, depending on your degree of understanding. The higher your understanding of reality, the better the reaction of reality will be in response to your needs.

You are immersed in it, just as it is immersed in you, in a continuum of causes and effects. So much so that you can't distinguish where you begin and where reality ends. And who knows if there really is a beginning and if there really is an end.

And what about nutrition? Have you thought about the decrease in sugar? Have you thought about how to get rid of that big square-headed monster called television?

Who knows how many thoughts are settling in you right now, and who knows how many good intentions you have put in a special closet, which you will be able to open at the right time. Because that's how it is, isn't it?

Even if you think "I can't do this and that," one day, who knows, your body, mind, and spirit will probably be so eager for harmony that they'll take back all the outstanding actions. They will gather all the attempts that have never begun, never defined, never finished, for fear of not being able to accomplish them. And that moment will mark the redemption from every supposed failure.

In the meantime, let's go back to our summary.

Have you started planning not to chase people anymore, to become the conductor of relationships?

Have you thought about the need to stop comparing your life to the lives of others?

Ah, and then there is the goal. The choice of only one goal to focus on. Well, I know that something moved in your mind when you read the word objective.

Your unconscious knows perfectly well what it wants. The trouble is to transfer it to your consciousness.

Communication is fallible: it's like a conversation between a man and a woman trying to say a sentence by gesticulating from behind a thick glass dulled by a thick fog.

The man will only get some shy, unintelligible signals. But who knows how many universes of meanings did the woman hide in those gestures hidden by the foggy residue?

If you are thinking about your limits, well, I can't help but remind you of the 40-60% rule, and the 80/20 principle.

Always keep them in a corner of your mind.

And when they escape your memory, take them back. You will need to go over them from time to time, believe me.

It's not easy to assimilate certain concepts from the very beginning; it's not easy to make them your own, to feel them, to resonate with them. This is why a good re-reading is needed because it will allow you to sink into the conceptual abyss of an inner transformation.

Before this text comes to an end, I want to thank you for having welcomed my writing into your mind, I want to thank you for having welcomed my words into your words, and I want to thank you for having welcomed me into your reality. Every time you connect to a language different than your own, you are expanding your perception.

Because in the act of connecting with the different, you are already experimenting with your own ways of perceiving the different from you.

When you study the Other from you, all you're doing is studying your own ways of studying the Other.

When you know the Other from you, all you're doing is knowing You.

Chapter 11: A first Overview of Emotions

Generally, when one approaches emotions, there's this tendency to start from the word's etymology. I want to start from its emoji.

Why daring so? It's very easy. Emojis are part of our daily communication.

And when they interpose between words, they're often valid to substitute words themselves, or they provide to disambiguate the intention of the whole speech.

In short, what are these yellowish faces that have the power to substitute words? Where does their communicative power come from?

Well, if you had to place a kid in front of an emoji or a word, you wouldn't have a doubt in believing that the kid would observe the emoji with more enthusiasm.

The child would immediately recognize the familiarity with the facial expression: he identifies eyes and mouth, embedded in the spheroidal of the face.

In two words: he identifies and recognizes himself in the emoji and therefore prefers it to the word.

Because he feels the emoji to be closer to him than the word.

So, maybe our spasmodic research of the meaningful, definitive, perfect emoji, is nothing more than a ploy to look for the one that resembles us, to find again our emotion, lost in the skein of all the faded feelings, thanks to the fact that – in the emojis keyboard – we see its projection outside of us.

Hence, emojis reflect the almost completed spectrum of our daily emotions, and it's like we were reminded of the existence of certain feelings while looking for them in the reflection of existence itself.

How many times does an emotion end up in oblivion just because you stopped feeling it?

Well, our emojis keyboard reminds us at the same time that it still exists, even if it no longer exists for you. It reminds us that the oblivion can be a transitory, transient condition and that all those emotions are still there and tell us "hey, here we are," while they only wait to be embodied, experienced, interpreted.

In front of emojis, we're like a child who identifies himself with the image of a doll with realistic somatic features.

But why do we depend on emotions?

Well, this is the best moment to be guided by the etymological review.

Emotion. E-motion. Move outside.

Let's analyze the word "move," and then we will analyze the word "outside." Afterward, I assure you, you'll understand the reasons for our addiction to emotions.

The movement is what allows to touch the extremes of anything. The movement is the satisfaction of curiosity: since only what moves from an extreme to another allows a thing to be grasped from every perspective. Think about it: could you ever say you knew a wonder if you had never known horror?

To move. What's shaken, what stirs **within** us, every time something moves **outside**.

It's a roundabout that reconciles the inside and the outside.

An emotion comes from the outside and hits the inside, or it comes from the inside and hits the outside.

And which act comes first, whether if the stimulus comes from within or without, is difficult to establish, since the process seems to be so interconnected not to allow the space of distinction among colors. It's a homogeneous whole in the form of a rainbow.

We depend on emotions to the extent that we depend on movement and curiosity.

The point is that emotions contribute to our spiritual and mental evolution from one side, and they also gift us with some experience, and constitute us as human beings. On the other side, they could get us involved and regress.

Running after a crumbling emotion is not that different from chasing after a ghost. And since the emotion is, because of its nature, crumbling, that is, destined to collapse under the pull of a new emotion, then we're risking running after ghosts for our whole life.

I mean, is there a bigger waste of time?

And the worst part is that the closer an emotion is ready to collapse, the more we're pushed by an irrational instinct that makes us want to save it from destruction.

Irrationality sums up to high irrationality, a vortex of dreams and nightmares, from which we can only escape by blocking the emotion.

It's not about erasing an emotion for good, but, well, it's actually about knowing how to handle the time it subtracts (or adds) to our lives.

It's about the path that every human being who wants to really evolve, who manages to deal with what seems to be apparently untamable.

Emotions seem to be untamable; it seems like we're always getting controlled by emotional clamor, and we have the visible evidence during fright, anger, and surprise. Acts and facts answer to our emotions. And our emotions guide what's unconscious and what's conscious.

Emotions seem to be untamable. But the good news is, they aren't.

And it can be testified by anyone who has, at least once in his life, learned to control the sudden emergence of a fear.

In the journey we're about to walk, get ready for a sort of objection from the ones who are not ready! Get ready to be asked: hey, don't you ever get emotional? When you are too good to dissimulate sorrow or happiness, without theatricalizing them with performances made up of screams, cries, laughs.

Get ready to get looks of suspicion and distrust.

In short, be ready to show your diversity among people who are used to emotional conformism.

But remember the reason for your journey:

If you ask for a positive reason for existence,

You must be able to control negative emotions.

You can't hope for a new, decent life as long as you remain a slave to your emotions. You can't take them as long as you'll be under the tenacious rule of your emotions.

And at this point, all you have to do is walking this second path together with me.

I promise you, I'll accompany you with the right delicacy and, when it will be necessary, with the right strength that will help you to get out from your slavery.

After all, nobody is going to tell you that getting out from something's domain means to let it go completely.

True peace is when you don't need to move to look for an emotion, it's when you don't need an *outside* anymore: in that exact moment, you'll realize that you don't look for it on the outside, because it's already within you.

Chapter 12: What Does Science Say About Emotions?

But now, let's see if science manages to give us a more formal description of emotions. And more importantly, let's see what the limits of science are when it tries to frame them.

You don't believe emotions can be reduced to a series of neuronal connections. I hope. Well, we perfectly know that the anatomical-functional substrate of emotions corresponds to a series of reactions that take place in our brain, but this shouldn't surprise us, because every state of consciousness has its neurologic counterpart!

And yet, the phenomenon of emotions **is not at all explainable in its enormous complexity** in terms of biochemical reactions.

Therefore, any attempt to explain every facet of a single emotion by simply observing what happens in our physical brain, well, is going to be vacuous, insufficient, incomplete.

Just because a phenomenon has its counterpart in the physical brain doesn't mean that the phenomenon itself is entirely **produced, originated, and organized** by the physical brain.

Don't forget that neurosciences have no evidence that consciousness is a product of the brain, and they never managed to prove efficaciously that the brain is not actually a mere filter of consciousness.

The fact that consciousness is situated in a certain physical place is not proof that it comes **from** that physical place.

Therefore, the same cognitive limit also concerns the mechanism of the genesis of emotions.

Saying that "if a specific area of the brain stops working, then a certain X emotion will be inhibited, and therefore that X emotion depends on that area of the brain" is not valid enough.

This is not valid as a conclusion, because if a filter becomes deformed, it's clear that water will no longer be able to flow in a linear fashion! So, if an area of the brain that **filters an emotion** stops being efficient, consequentially the emotion will encounter resistance and difficulty to transfer outside.

Many people, unluckily, give up hope to the possibility that there's a non-physic consciousness, independent from the physical brain.

And do you know when all of this happens?

It happens when people witness the cognitive decline of a relative. For example, people with Alzheimer's, senile dementia, and the whole range of diseases that determine a depletion of mental faculties.

This phenomenon of resignation and total distrust in a non-physic dimension is perfectly understandable.

When we see it only takes a scratch on the brain to ruin the entire building of someone's memories; when the person we have loved the most in our lives doesn't remember our face, our name, our hands, it's almost inevitable to doubt the eternity of love.

Love. Speaking of love.

I want to tell you something that you may not have been made aware of yet.

There's a very rare, I'd say almost exceptional, phenomenon called **terminal lucidity.**

When this phenomenon takes place, something incredible and inexplicable – according to the parameters of official medicine – happens!

The patient before dying starts to recover memories, habits, feelings, that everyone thought he had lost because of the irreversible damages to the brain.

And yet... with the amazement of the families, patients who experiment the phenomenon of terminal lucidity reawaken as if they had never lost their memories! It's truly exceptional.

This phenomenon is not relatively new: there are some historical testimonies dating back to the times of the writer Giambattista Vico.

I suggest you to read his biography, which clarifies how the author experienced terminal lucidity, witnessed by his children.

I gave you this example to illustrate the equivocal nature of the cause-effect relationship under these circumstances.

Let's limit to accept the scientific description as a part of the explanation of emotions, and not as the cognitive exhaustion of that explanation.

What is an emotion, according to science?

Let's immediately start by pointing out that interpretations are not unique. Several scientists have elaborated interpretations of the phenomenology of emotions.

For example, in Darwinian terms, emotions are functional to make more efficient the individual's survival, thanks to emotional reactions to threatening events.

One of the most interesting aspects of emotions is the somatic effect that comes directly from the psyche. The **symptom**.

We can see the invisible becoming visible thanks to the symptom.

In fact, the emotion produces a series of somatic changes, among them: the oscillation of the heart rate, the intensity of sweating, acceleration or slowing of the respiratory rate, stiffening or relaxation of muscle districts, and even the enlargement or decrease in the diameter of the pupils.

Therefore, an emotion gets so many expressive ways on the human body that we are terribly fascinated by it. It's curious, isn't it?

Even when we are fascinated by something, emotions are in charge: hence, we get emotional by the sight of our own emotions.

It must be said that scientists tend to make a distinction between emotions and feelings: emotions would be the **immediate** response of our brain; feelings would be the **conscious elaboration** of the emotion we've felt.

In short, science tells us that emotions could live by themselves, even without our further reflections.

But then, how should we interpret it when people tell us we are… emotional people?

Why do people say "emotional person" when what they mean is "sensible person"?

If emotions are independent of people's self-reflection, then do they have an active or passive role in determining the intensity of their emotions?

Here's where we start delineating the limits of scientific research in this regard: these implications are, at best, psychological and philosophical.

You can formulate your hypothesis.

Think about yourself and your relationship with your emotions.

What's your hypothesis?

Are you your emotions' owner?

Do you succeed in controlling them?

Do you get to amplify them?

Have you ever asked yourself if other people feel emotions weaker than you do?

As you can see, there's a lot to discuss about emotions. Even if right now we're busy creating a feeling (...since we're reflecting on emotions), it doesn't matter.

The result of this reflection could lead you along the abyss of your emotional roots, and perhaps it will allow you to control and shape your reactions to certain environmental stimuli that are generally difficult to control.

Chapter 13: Definitions, Interpretations, and Misinterpretations of the Ego

Ego.

How many times have you heard pronouncing this magic word in the most disparate contexts?

And who knows how many times it has been completely distorted in its original meaning, just because it seems to be so fashionable to talk about the ego.

After all, maybe you've noticed it, the ones who fill their mouths with practices meant to deflate the ego are the exact same ones who are looking to inflate their egos by getting approval for those… ego-deflating theories!

Yes, I know, it's an intricate round of actions and reactions, but it's more common than you might expect.

Maybe you've heard the best explanation of the ego-deflation from people who have been silent.

And I'm not here to tell you something absolute about the ego, I just want to tell you something about its interpretations.

The most supplied fields of knowledge are the psychoanalytical, spiritual, and neuroscientific ones.

And it's interesting noticing that each of these fields of knowledge contextualizes the word "ego" differently.

Classical psychoanalysis, starting with Freud, conceives the ego as a balancing tool, as if it was the bearer of harmony between the tendencies of instincts (Es) and those of duties (Super Ego). Therefore, the ego assumes an essentially positive meaning.

Despite this, when we get closer to a more spiritualistic approach in psychoanalysis, we notice how the ego's function starts changing. In fact, according to Jung, the ego is not the center of our psyche, but just one of the components of a bigger whole. **The center of the psyche would no longer be the ego, but the unconscious.**

And here we are, approaching the highest peaks of spirituality, where the positive function of the ego starts fading away slowly, where the presence of the ego becomes almost unwieldy, as if to fill a negative and hindering meaning.

The ego starts being a specter, a false and illusory shade that distracts us constantly, that drags us away from our true nature, that hinders our spiritual evolution.

It's not the bearer of harmony anymore: it becomes the great bearer of disharmony.

The ego becomes the unbalancing tendency, since it consolidates the identity, and since **the more we identify, the more we separate**, the ego reinforces in men the illusory belief of their separation from the whole.

The spiritual definition of ego is the sense of the Self, the perception of being someone, a fallacious belief that can lead us far away from our real Self, because it makes us feel separate from our real essence, from God, from everything that ever was and will eternally be, the pure Being.

The more we get far from neurosciences and psychology, the more we get closer to the negative meaning of the ego.

But how can one eviscerate the real meaning of the ego? Where can it be grasped clearly?

First of all, let's try to remove the words **egoism** and **egocentrism** from confusion and equivocation. As you can see, both words have the prefix ego- in common, but throughout the reading you'll realize that they are two completely different concepts both in meaning and application.

There's a tendency to confuse these words. Which are the real differences? And most importantly, how useful is egoism and how useful is egocentrism?

It could be said that egoism is a behavioral modality typical of people who tend to take care only of themselves, not caring about others' desires, needs, and requests.

And what about egocentrism? Egocentrism is a little bit more complex to frame. In some ways it's even "normal" (meaning that it's not condemnable) when we're kids!

In fact, according to the most famous psychologists, egocentrism is a natural tendency for children.

But let's see... what exactly does it consist of?

Egocentrism is a classical attitude of people who tend to refer everything to themselves, implanting themselves (...as they say) at the center of the world. They're static people, we could say, right?

Since they don't pay any attention to other people's points of view, it's like egocentric people lived perennially cooped up in the same little corner of the room, giving up to any perspective because of their inability to move.

The real question is whether this renounce is conscious or unconscious.

That is, does an egocentric know that he's missing out on three-quarters of the panorama of that room? Or does he believe that the panorama of the room is exhausted in that little corner?

I believe it's the second one.

An egocentric has no idea what he's missing out, because if he knew, he would immediately stop being one.

Even kids don't realize the damages produced by egocentrism, do they?

So, who knows if the adult egocentric is not an individual who has not yet passed the stage of childhood egocentrism, almost as if he or she was literally stuck in that phase.
Have you ever wondered about that?

One thing is sure, anyway.

Even the most egocentric man can't do without the Other. Any center, by definition, needs a space around it.

Maybe the right spiritual direction of the word **ego** is not in error, as it may be at first glance.

If the ego forces us to a situation of separateness so stifling that we're unable to look beyond the corner of our room, where's the balance? Where's the balance that the ego should bring? Maybe we simply don't know how to use its real function: that of a **tempter**.

If our ego **tempts** us continuously to the division, to the splitting from the Whole, it means that the ego has a huge role in setting in motion the greatest challenge of our lives.

And that is, **striving for union despite everything.**

Despite the sense of competition, despite the divergence of forms, of the color of the skin, of ideas and ideologies, of opinions and beliefs, of languages and writings, of perceptions and misperceptions, of economic, social, cultural statuses, political parties and fan base.

Despite the diversities that hovers in the air and seem to want to substitute the communion of our feeling, despite the ego's structures make us identify with the mask we wear to be in the world, despite all this, we tend to One.

The ego is fundamental because only through **temptation** we can measure the intensity of our **intention**.

The intention to go back to the truth.

They always made us believe that altruism was a sort of duty. They say that if you're altruist, you're good, if you're egoist, you're bad.

I say it's about being intelligent.

And you know why? The altruistic impulse derives from the sense of injustice. Period.

If you're intelligent enough to realize you're living in a world of injustice, you can't help but walking the path of altruism.

Try to prove me wrong.

As soon as you realize that you have something that someone else doesn't have, and you commit until they get the same privileges that you already have, well, that's not a duty, it's not about being good: it's about being balanced.

It's the irresistible supreme intelligence that wants to put in order the damage of a pre-existing disorder. And do you have this supreme intelligence that generates and guides your altruistic acts?

Don't ever think about being a bad person because you don't have the impulse to do good, from time to time. Good is not always an impulse.

Good needs to be tasted, savored; it must be known to be recognized as Good.

Listen. When you start doing good for other people, even if at the beginning it will be just coldly desired on your part, I can assure you that at a certain point, even after a long time, that desire to do good will be a necessity for you, a visceral need like feeding yourself.

Because yes, you'll start feeding yourself with the smiles you create in others, in the positive emotions you create in them, in the happy endings you create for them.

Hey, don't give up because of that time you thought, "if I don't have the impulse of giving money to this beggar, it means I'm a bad person." You weren't! You aren't!

You're not, for the simple fact that you recognized the error, you recognized the injustice and the unbalance.

Where was the fault? It was in the laziness of your intelligence.

When your intelligence becomes supreme intelligence, you'll be able to do anything that is above your expectations.

Why don't you start just now?

Supreme intelligence doesn't develop on its own! It wants to be stimulated by your actions.

I'll say that again. Sow good wherever you go. Especially to strangers. Yes, especially to them. You have to go exactly where you think you can't go.

This attitude will allow you to break mental walls, all the limits you've always built throughout your life. Go and sow some good.

Go out. Look for people in need. And if you find one, comfort him with the same words that once comforted you.

You'll be each step towards the Other you take, closer and closer to the Infinite and Unitary Essence of which you're a part.

Chapter 14: How Do Words Impact Emotions?

If you believe that words can't determine intense emotions, well, I bet you won't hesitate to change your mind when I explain the placebo and nocebo effect.

The placebo and nocebo effect not only show that words determine more or less intense emotions, but they show that even **words radically change our perception of reality and our reality.**

But let's go step by step and see how words can determine relatively simple emotions.

Have you ever blushed at a compliment?

Or have you ever felt a sense of constriction, or fire, or emptiness, in the pit of your stomach, just when the person you like has said **words** of some value to you?

Well, then you have experienced on your skin (...literally) the change of emotions determined by the choice of words.

After all, what are words?

Aren't they sounds that encompass meanings?

Think about it: if a **meaningless** sound like the basis of a wordless song can – all alone – make you feel sadder, more nostalgic, more dreamy, happier, then imagine what could a **meaningful** sound do!

Which is? Nothing more, nothing less than a **word**.

And then tell me: how many times have you cried at a movie? And how many times have you laughed out loud because of a joke?

Well, a well-written joke is just a mix of graphic signs, if you think about it!

And yet, it produced a series of biochemical reactions in your brain that have translated into a thunderous laugh. What do you say? Isn't this magic?

Wait, wait a minute. If it's true that laughter is capable of generating a production of hormones, and if it's true that hormones are scientifically detectable, does this mean that **words have a direct impact on our organism as well?**

Can a sound change the biochemistry in our body?

Well, yes. Can you see how words' magic is gradually arising and intensifying more and more?

You'll be probably asking yourself what the placebo and nocebo effect have to do with this. Actually, there is an interesting bond among all the things we've said up to now.

I'll try to explain myself. Studies have been conducted on the ways some hospitalized patients react, and scientists have noticed a few things:

1) Patients who were told reassuring, empathic, motivational, optimistic words responded better to therapy than patients who were given neutral words.

2) When a doctor used words reinforcing the belief in the curative power of a particular drug (...or placebo), patients responded

better to therapies than patients who were not mentioned by any doctor about the effectiveness of therapies.

These two points deserve a lot of attention.

And do you know why?

Because they give us insight into how much word conditioning can even determine response to therapy. Get the picture.

It seems like we're in front of pure medicines (words), to which we add classic medicines.

It's as if words could determine the healing of a person. Without disturbing miracles. I'd say this is already prodigious.

It's like words had the same active ingredient of drugs. And maybe now you're wondering: where can this active ingredient be found?

Just saying. What's the active ingredient in the word Love?

Well. In chemistry, the active ingredient is the component of the drugs on which its curative action depends. Therefore, the active ingredient of words must be the component of the meaning from which its curative action depends.

In short, the active ingredient of a word must be found in a meaning of the word itself, in the meaning that most commonly gets to heal someone from a malaise.

Love.

What's the active ingredient of this word?

Perhaps it is the memory of a particular situation in your life in which you've felt love. If it is so, then its active ingredient acts on memory, it dusts off memories. And it means that the curative meaning doesn't belong to the word, but to the personal meaning you've given to that word.

It's not the word love that saves, but the interpretation you've given to the word love. It's not love that saves, but the interpretation you've given to love.

So, is it true that the most authentic medicine is contained within us already?

In short, if the interpretation of things is a purely internal matter, and if the interpretation of a word caused it to perform a healing action, it means that we literally invented the cure.

Sure, we leaned on a horizon of meanings that were already objectively known, but the personalized sense of the word Love was felt in our subjective horizon.

We added sense to sense.

Maybe that's why we are constantly bombarded by that phrase that goes "if you believe, then it will work!" or that other related phrase that goes "if you have faith, then it will work!" I don't know, what do you think?

I mean, I mean, even faith is a purely internal thing... Just like the subjective interpretation of a word.

And what is the connection between faith in God and faith in the interpretation of a word?

You know, I'd like to reveal a little linguistic quandary of mine: when we write, we inevitably rely on our own interpretations.

It's not that we stop and say: wait, is this the true meaning of the word I'm writing? No. Somehow, we just believe it.

And this trusty attitude towards our interpretation of words is wrong, on one side, because it doesn't make us put under discussion our certainties (we don't know if we might have misunderstood the meaning). On the other side, it allows us to write without interruptions.

Confidence in our interpretation of words allows us to write continuously, without fears or suspensions.

Kind of like when trusting God allows us to live without pauses of skepticism and the suspensions of life's meaning.

Even if this is not completely right: for what concerns me, we need **real** skepticism to get to the **truth**.

However, when we have overcome the skeptic phase, the act of faith shouldn't be restrained.

This is what happens when trusting the meaning of words.

You question your certainties on the meaning of words, re-interpret them if it's the case, but when skepticism is over, I warn you: have faith in your interpretation.

Let's get back to the nocebo effect now.

The nocebo effect makes us understand how the active ingredients of words are also toxic.

The term active ingredient indicates a substance with a certain biological activity and includes all substances with a therapeutic (drugs), beneficial (vitamins, probiotics) or toxic (poisons) effect.

So yes, words have just as abundant a therapeutic active ingredient as they do a toxic active ingredient.

Beneficial words are just as powerful as poisonous words.

So how does the nocebo effect work?

Imagine. Dr. Z tells patient X that he is about to receive a medication. Patient X does not seem at all upset by the news.

However, before administering it to him, Dr. Z. warns his patient about the potential side effects of that medication.

And suddenly Patient X begins to show some expressions of restlessness on his face. About ten minutes after administering the drug, Patient X starts sweating, has hot flashes scattered all over, chills, nausea, and gags.

Oh, no! These are just some of the side effects that Dr. Z. had just explained to him!

Okay. Now let's take a little step back.

Dr. Z. smiles.

Huh? What the hell is he smiling about? Can't he see that the patient is having a bad reaction to the medication?

He shyly approaches patient X.

He speaks to him, merely murmuring these innocent words: son, do you know that I only gave you a little water and talcum powder?

Silence.

Thoughts stop. There was no medication in Patient X's blood. Just water and talcum powder.

Symptoms disappear within ten minutes. Patient X breathes a sigh of relief.
But when he reenters his lucid state, he can't help but think: how great is the power of autosuggestion?

And you, who just read this story: can you tell me how great the power of autosuggestion is?

Faith in reassuring words does as much good as faith in alarming words does bad.

No difference in intensity.

The Bad you receive from distressing words doesn't differ in intensity from the Good that you receive from happy words.

Sure, there are people who receive Good more than Bad, or the contrary, according to what impresses them the most. But in general, the active ingredient works exactly in the same way, whether it turns in the direction of Bad or in the direction of Good.

Maybe you've been the X patient in the past.

Maybe you're afraid of becoming one.

Or perhaps you think you already are, unconsciously.

Well, let me tell you something: patient X had no idea he had a great power.

Exactly as he could yield to the suggestion of evil, so he could yield to the suggestion of good.

And you know what happens when Mr. X succumbs to the suggestion of good?

The cure works.

Chapter 15: How Does the Environment Impact Your Emotions?

A sunset, a summer evening, a light autumn breeze, a snowstorm, a sight in the frost, the cyclic alternation of the seasons, the different combination of colors, landscapes that become mental photographs.

Have you ever felt even a single emotion about any of these things?

I bet you did.

Isn't it curious that we get emotional in front of these natural phenomena? I mean, we are nature, and yet we get emotional in front of nature.

It's like nature looked at itself in the mirror and got emotional by seeing itself.

But then, a question arises for me spontaneously: why is it that all this whirlwind of emotions never catches us at the sight of our body, face, mind?

Why do we only get emotional in front of our **external** nature, and not to the one **within** ourselves?

May it be that when we always have something in front of our eyes, this thing becomes boring and inevitably stops surprising us? So, is this the fate of our body in front of our gaze?

Sometimes, I believe we should re-learn everything we've learnt throughout our lives, just so we can still surprise ourselves with everything we re-learn.

And who knows, we may not have already done this billions of times, every time, before we incarnated on earth.

Relearning everything just for the beauty to be surprised again. It would be a nice gimmick to avoid boredom, wouldn't it?

And who knows, we may not have already done this billions of times, every time, before we incarnated on earth.

Unlearning everything just for the beauty of surprising ourselves with the new. That would be a nice gimmick to avoid boredom, wouldn't it?

And maybe the whole life would be reduced to a series of gimmicks, strategically designed just to avoid the risk of being bored!

It sounds absurd, but I bet that this doesn't sound so far from your usual intentions. Think about it: aren't we humans always fighting against boring situations? Aren't we constantly trying to escape boring situations?

All this fear, all this fear of boredom, must have its roots somewhere, in some remote time, in some remote space, who knows where, who knows when and how, who knows why.

Everything is, probably, in understanding if these roots also define the very tree of human existence, that is, if boredom is the universal feeling that is both origin, extension and end, or if the roots of boredom exist only to allow us to develop other feelings.

No, maybe not feelings. But **emotions**, precisely. Yes, in this sense, boredom would exist only as a function of the emergence of a variety of alternative emotions, which would not be able to emerge without the backdrop of boredom.

Boredom as a backdrop for emotions, how about that?

A still void that must be filled with movement. And when the void is filled with movement, emotion is generated. Emotion has within it the meaning of **movement**.

So, we need to look lovingly at even the fixed and boring things because they allow us to go **through** and **through them**, and the only way to do that is to constantly create emotional and exciting scenarios.

Getting excited in front of a starry sky, after centuries of poetry about starry skies, seems trivial, very trivial. But is it so?

Where is the philosophical meaning of this emotional current? Why do we emote in front of something that is connatural to the structure of the universe, as connatural as we are? Why does the starry sky not appear repugnant to us?

Yet, there are so many natural things down here that move the emotion of revulsion and disgust!

How come this negative emotion never projects into things up there?

It may be that the more distant something is from us, the more we see that thing as perfect for the simple fact that it is far from our imperfection. So, is getting excited about a starry sky insecurity?

And again: is it really the things that are fascinating and repulsive, or are we the ones who throw onto **external** things the fascination and repugnance we already have **inside**?

Do things give us emotions, or do we give emotions to things?

It is clear that perhaps too sharp a split is not possible here. It's possible for there to be a coexistence, some correspondence, a mixing, between what we already have inside and throw on the things outside, and what the things outside move us inside. It's not, so to speak, a one-way action, but it's a two-way relationship, between us and things, between the human being and the environment.

So, to the question, what is the relationship between our emotions and the environment?

We should replace the questions: what is our relationship to the environment? Are we really separate from the environment or are we ourselves the environment?

Thus, the origin of emotions would certainly be less ambiguous, clearer, because it would come from something unique. If there is a correspondence between projected emotions and introjected emotions, then maybe we are not two separate entities, we and the environment, the environment and us, but we are an inseparable unit that moves in two different spaces, that has two different locations, and that continuously exchanges information just for the sake of communication.

Emotions are the least elaborate and paradoxically most sought-after communication tool of all: we communicate to ourselves, and to others, with our emotions, even when we are completely still and silent.

It's a fact: emotions are moved even by real estate.

The vault of heaven seems motionless and yet there is still that great tradition of getting excited by the color of the sky.

Who knows how this is possible? Who knows where the engine of emotion is located, and who knows if we have it inside us or if it is independent of our inner universe? Who knows if there is a real separation between our inner universe and the universe outside us?

So many questions are moved by the movement of emotion. As you can see, the banality of getting excited in front of the starry sky has given rise to a sequence of philosophical questions that are anything but banal.

Remember this well, when someone tells you that you are saying or doing something trivial. Tell them: yes, maybe I am saying or doing something banal, but only to allow you to elaborate something original starting from the absence of originality. I hand over the void of originality to allow you to fill it.

Chapter 16: How Do Emotions Form?

Well, first of all, to start talking about something that gets formed, we have to be sure that that thing has a form.

Do emotions have one? If yes, which one? Or maybe they have several ones.

Maybe one single emotion has many forms, as it can be interpreted in many ways.

Or maybe it has no form, because it has no clear, precise, well defined boundaries.

I ask you to choose now.

Which alternative are you inclined to believe? Form or formless?

Let's suppose emotions really get formed. How do they do it? What's their original source?

Someone, maybe some scientist, would say that they get formed into our brains. Someone else, maybe some philosopher, would say that they form in the space of interaction between mind and matter. Someone, maybe some philosopher of a Platonic orientation, would say that an emotion forms in an unearthly place, a divine one, and any emotion on earth is just the imitation of an emotion that arises in a divine place.

Someone, maybe a linguist, would say that an emotion gets formed as soon as we communicate it to someone, because it's just in the word itself that one can form the formless.

Everyone has something to say about the nature of the emotion, but who has ever found this phantomatic nature of the emotion?

Maybe it's right this way. In this regard, maybe it's fine if we don't find it. This is the way we get a little space to interpret.

What a big disgrace it would be if someone handed over to us the absolute truth once and for all!

What would be of our little partial truths? Of our attempts of getting closer to the absolute truth with such daring.

When the truth comes, you have to be ready to say goodbye to the desire for truth.

No matter how hard we try to demand absolute truth, probably we're not ready to renounce the desire for the research.

And who can tell that? It's possible that we're facing this tortuous earthly path precisely because, out of the fear for absolute truth, we preferred living in illusion.

We have chosen the illusion because it was the only way to continue to desire.

A game, all things considered.

But is the game worth the candle?

Is the game of illusion worthy, even if the earthly illusion includes all this pain, all this injustice, all this horror?

It's like someone was forcing us to choose to come to terms with the negative and the positive, if we wished to continue desiring.

This way, the desire feeds itself with opposites.

How do emotions form?

Now you have clearer ideas, I guess. Or more confused than before. But it doesn't really matter. What matters is that you now have ideas that you didn't have before. It matters that you have new ideas, which will produce other new ideas; because that's how it works when you start thinking about something innovative, the process doesn't stop easily, and it keeps on going until you consume all the breath of the thoughts, which clumsily translate the insights.

The intuition of how emotions form is personal, I want you to decide for yourself their form.

What's even more interesting, more than their forms, it's their information.

After wondering about the way they form, one should ask how they inform.

Is an emotion, an information?

Yes, it's an information.

If I manifest the signs of sadness on my face because I feel sad, then I'm **informing** the ones who are around me that I'm feeling a certain type of emotion.

The emotion gets channelized by my face; it becomes an expression and informs the observers.

In the same way, it informs me as well.

The emotion tells me that something inside of me is still capable of stirring. It's still able to move. E-motion. To move.

I'm informed by my own emotion, because an emotion uttered on the face, or gathered in a trembling voice, or in an impulsive gesture, informs me that the emotion really exists and is making its course through the aisles of the body.

Therefore, an emotion really is an information.

There's a current of thought, quite peculiar, it must be admitted, that believes that all things in the world, from objects to plants and water, can be informed by our thoughts and emotions. That is, it's like we imprint our thoughts and emotions on these objects with our closeness, or maybe with concentration, or because of an emotional bond of some depth.

And here we go again with the emotion-information.

They say, in fact, that these objects, once conditioned by our thoughts and our emotions, we send everything back to us with a greater energy! For example, if one day you feel happy and hold an object in your hands, transferring consciously that happiness, well, if after a month you'll be deeply sad and discouraged, you just need to take that object to re-absorb all the happiness it absorbed from you.

It's a swinging and fluctuating give-and-take.

There's an exchange of information between you and the object, but you're the one who gets to decide what type of information you want to imprint on the object. The object is a transceiver.

It's a passive receiver of your information.

And it's an active transmitter of your information.

It receives and releases. It absorbs and drips.

Imagine a sponge that instead of filling itself with water, fills itself with information. But here you are, now something's crossing my mind.

If an object can be a sponge absorbing negative information, can it happen by chance that **you could also be a sponge, absorbing negative information?**

If so, you should be very careful about being around those who complain, those who swear, those who rant, those who envy, those who sigh with regret, repentance, guilt.

Yes, you should stay away from the ones who transfer, even unconsciously, negative information to you. Because, just like a transceiver object, that information could imprint itself on your brain, and download directly to your body.

How many times have you felt a sense of trembling because someone in your surroundings was nervous?

If it happened to you, it's possible that you are more sensitive to these manifestations of... emotional information.

Chapter 17: Emotions Can Be the Compass Guiding Your Path

Has it ever happened to you that you felt suddenly lost, or concerned, or scared when you reached a new place?

Well, if we try to deeply analyze this emotion of bewilderment, concern, or fear, we'd notice that it could have a double meaning.

The first meaning concerns an old memory that the place reminded you of, maybe that place smelled like another place that traumatized you; or maybe a geometric form superimposed to the form that was in front of you during a traumatic moment, or a sound, or a hissing of leaves, a noise of the gate, or the front door.

In short, any symbol coming from that place could have unlocked the key to a dramatic event, that maybe your unconscious removed from your conscience to take a burden away.

In this regard, as you might guess, **emotions** played a fundamental role.

Think about it: thanks to the presence of that emotion that manifested exactly in a specific place you visited for the first time; you can be pushed to retrieve the traumatic event that the place has evoked.

Thanks to the emotion provoked from that place, you can head into the meanders of your unconscious to discover yourself. So, we can say that **emotion can be the compass that guides us in the right direction.**

On one side, facing the malaise makes you want to run away; but on the other side, it makes you wonder: why?

Why are you feeling so bad in that place? What's wrong with it? What's wrong with you, relating to that place?

Questions travel all around and move from subject to object. Who moved that emotion?

The place, the energy, or maybe my dark memory, which was looking for a way out?

The bad memory is only waiting for you to get in touch with some other badness to feel at home and go out to take a walk.

This is how an ugly memory begins feeling comfortable if you make it see another ugliness. The memory of evil begins feeling comfortable if you let it see some more evil.

Whether the evil is a shape, a color, or a smell… who cares? What matters is that in that moment, you're being receptive.

And if something is stirring in you, no matter what type of emotion, it means you're receptive. It means you can dig into your hell in search of the unfinished business with yourself.

Yes, an emotion, just a single emotion, can lead you the way to reach your weakest point, the burning flame that has been silently burning under your consciousness for who knows how long.

One single emotion can be the engine behind your personalized psychotherapy, where you are the researcher, the doctor, and the patient of yourself.

Can you see how wonderful the guide of an emotion is?

But let's deal with positive emotions now.

For example, you're practicing a particular type of meditation and at a certain point you feel a positive emotion, don't ignore it or don't forget it soon after.

That positive emotion is still a compass, exactly like the negative emotion is.

The positive emotion shows you the right way to be happy. Therefore, make sure you always keep it in a well-placed corner of your mental post-its.

Every time you'll feel empty, as if something was missing, as if you were looking for something somewhere, try to do exactly what gave you that positive emotion!

And if it was meditation, what are you waiting for?

Get back on track, put yourself in the same position as then, focus the same way, and get ready to feel the same positive emotion, the same serenity again.

Thanks to it, you could learn and understand what makes you feel good.

An emotion is a didactic tool.

Have you ever thought about it?

Learning from our own emotions is like studying from the book of our brain and organism. It's a true field experiment, of all the theory we see told in the best manuals on the market, about how the brain and emotions work.

Isn't it exciting (… just to stay on topic), being able to study our own emotions?

Sure, to study them adequately, that is, without the emotion being distorted by the presence of the emotion itself, a bit of emotional detachment is needed. It's important one projects himself outside of him for a little bit of time, already knowing the way to get in again, but richer. Collecting vacuous emotions isn't a good method to know what makes us emotional negatively or positively.

Each emotion needs to be clarified in order to be proposed in moments of need.

But don't forget that negative emotions don't always signal a situation from which we should run away. Even negative emotions can do some good.

Think about when you have to take a bitter syrup. What do you feel?

Definitively disgust. A sickening emotion.

And yet, behind that emotion there's a form of healing.

So, following the same principle, don't be afraid of the painful emotions that you're going to face in your life. They're probably healing something you can't see with your eyes, hear with your ears, and touch with your hands.

But they're healing, something's healing, against all odds from your unpleasant emotions.

Emotions can be a compass, yes, but they can also be a deceptive one. They make us believe something is not working when it's actually working very well.

I know it might sound like an aberrant contradiction, but there are too many things that work like that in nature.

And when a path repeats itself so many times, it's evident that that path is predicted by nature just like it presents itself to us.

Whether seemingly paradoxical or not, that path is preset by a law of nature that we can only write down in notes to **remind us of how the environment works, and how we work in relation to the environment.**

Chapter 18: How Emotion Can Help Us in Our Personal Growth

Human emotions, according to new scientific research, are far more numerous than once believed.

Until a few years ago, there was a consensus that there were four universal emotions: joy, sadness, anger and fear.

Today, things seem to have changed. The emotions have been categorized into a more extensive list, including admiration, surprise, adoration, anxiety, aesthetic appreciation, fear, embarrassment, calm, confusion, boredom, desire, disgust, empathic pain, envy, enchantment, excitement, fear, horror, interest, happiness, nostalgia, love, sadness, satisfaction, sexual desire, empathy, and exultation.

Now let's try to consider how these emotions can affect our personal growth journey.

Admiration.

Can admiration help us grow?

I say it can.

Think about it: when we admire someone, we tend to extol all their positive qualities. We appreciate him, esteem him, because we recognize his value. It doesn't matter what type of value, what matters is that that value is worthy of our admiration. Well, growth certainly comes by the phase of admiration.

One grows to become like an admired person.

Or maybe one grows when it's clear that even this admired person can earn our disdain in a second if he makes a mistake.

Or one grows when he gets out of the deception of idealization, which we often sew on ourselves in order to deeply admire someone that perhaps doesn't deserve a deep admiration. And then we idealize, we idealize, until shallow admiration conquers the step of deep admiration.

Growth is inevitable when we clash against that person's limits, or that thing's limits that we have been admiring for who knows how long. And suddenly, its limits become our own limits.

We have the feeling of time crumbling before our eyes, the feeling of wasted time, of time that could have been spent differently, perhaps better, perhaps much better. We grow together with the time that descends, in the shortening of time that separates us from the future.

Surprise.

What about surprise? Can it make us grow?

Indeed. Every time we are surprised by something, our gaze recognizes something new. Of course, we can also be surprised by something we already know, but the moment we are surprised, it means that we're getting to know the old in a **new** way.

This **new** way to perceive something is experience: the perceptual experience that sums up leads to a growth. Don't you agree?

Being surprised at the sight of news is easy, and everyone succeeds at it, more or less. But getting surprised at the sight of a known thing that we ourselves make new is something else.

It's authentic growth: knowing how to give an innovative and lively color to a faded hue.

Anxiety.

Can you thrive on anxiety? Brace yourself. You may not like this news. Or it may be especially comforting to you, depending on your temperament.

You grow faster through anxiety than through serenity.

Anxiety is pure, absolute, total movement: because it is a symptom that moves and is moved. It's **moved** by an event, a stimulus, an environmental or inner suggestion. And it **moves**, it starts by stirring inside of you, moves your organs, heartbeat, the frequency of your breathing, the contraction of your muscles; it agitates you, moves you, moves you literally.

And again, you also move to run from it, when you feel its restless, tormenting, cramped movement.

It's a circular movement that chases itself and runs from itself.

What's your side?

Are you chasing after or are you running away?

Anxiety makes you grow simply because you get to manage it only if you're already grown.

If your shoulders aren't strong enough, you can't handle the weight of anxiety. If you have anxiety and can handle it in some way, you've already grown. Without a shadow of a doubt. In short, growth is built-in to the appearance of anxiety.

And how often do you grow out of anxiety! You grow in unsuspected ways!

You grow up every time you start looking for a coping strategy; you grow up every time you give up something because you know that that something would make your anxiety increase. Because yes, sacrificing something so as not to exacerbate your anxiety means recognizing a Greater Good to what you are sacrificing: your peace of mind.

If you recognize a greater value to your serenity than to, I don't know, a formal dinner with your unbearable colleagues, it means you've grown.

If the dinner with your colleagues is just a formality, a façade and appearance vice, you just don't go, because you know your anxiety would only increase **and you prefer to give up form rather than substance.**

Because you have truly understood what are the important things for which it's worth to take a pause, interrupt the path, turning, change direction.

You're growing by seeing the evolution or the involution of anxiety.

Or you're growing suppressing the growth of anxiety.

Yes, maybe growing means preventing anxiety to grow with you.

Embarrassment.

What about it? Can it help us grow?

I think it can. Every time we feel embarrassed, we're placed in front of a question: why does this make me feel embarrassed?

If you ask yourself this question, you will discover that an inexhaustible horizon of possible answers will open up before your eyes. Embarrassment can have its source of meaning in childhood, in family or school conditioning, or in social conditioning, in the influences of films, books, social networks, or an idol. Embarrassment can be a distortion or concealment of another feeling. For example, how often do we say the phrase: I feel embarrassed to write first to the person I like.

Are we sure that emotion is embarrassment?

Or is embarrassment just the synthesis of a more elaborate and complex emotion? What if instead it can be framed in your **fear** of coming across as unpleasant, intrusive, cumbersome? Fear that that person won't appreciate your attempt to write to them. Willingness and desire that that person will be the first to give you a nice thought, because maybe you feel insecure and need security, even if only with a message.

Growing means understanding that maybe we have in front of us someone who might be even more insecure of us.

Because yes, I mean, who tells you that the person from whom you're expecting a reassurance isn't even more in need than you are?

Growing means to identify with the person we see as the source of our embarrassment, or our fear of not being enough.

Identifying is not easy. It's anything but easy.

And this is why it's necessary to grow.

How can you identify with someone if you're still too fragmented, even for yourself?

Before you identify with someone, you have to get a certain inner compactness. It doesn't have to be perfect: this needs to be clear. But you have to be sufficiently amalgamated to allow your thought to enter someone else's thought, without coming out even more fragmented, destroyed in smaller and smaller pieces.

You have to be strong if you want to deal with identification.

Here's all. Entering the cognitive and emotional dominion of others' is not for everybody. You have to be strong enough to get out of it without resulting compromised, sad, angry.

A certain emotional detachment is necessary. Even if it will paradoxically mix with the other's emotions.

Distancing and insertion.

Maybe distancing is a fundamental ingredient for an identification without side effects.

It's an abstract distancing, almost metaphorical, it's about being neutral, without prejudices, without being judging, nosy, intrusive, excessively curious about other people's business.

Think about it: would you like someone to identify with yourself just to be nosy? I think you wouldn't. Therefore, a good identification needs a pure transfer of consciousness.

You can start practicing even if your involvement is bonded to emotions: nobody will stop you. But know that, sooner or later, with some practice, you'll manage to understand what the flaws in your identification are.

And at that point, you'll be forced to **grow**, because growth will be the only choice you'll have. Growing will be the only alternative to darkness and insufficiency.

Boredom.

Does it help you grow?

Boredom, precisely because it manifests in the absence of stimuli, is a stimulus to grow. It seems a contradiction, but I want you to think about it without paying too much attention to the formal side of the reflection.

When you're bored, and you feel it to be negative, the desire to get out of it arises. You want to get out of it.

But before getting out, you can't help but wonder:

Why does this place bore me?

Why does this person bore me?

Why does this job bore me?

Why does this situation bore me?

You review all the external circumstances that may have contributed to the emergence of your boredom, and as soon as you can catch the culprit, that's when your life can really change, can radically transform, if you're able to recognize who is (or what) the executioner of your boredom.

And you start eliminating unnecessary items, cutting inconclusive relationships, leaving routine places, looking for new jobs, new ambitions. You start looking for newness.

And when you're alone with yourself, and still thinking, *I'm bored!* Then there will be something within you that demands renewal.

Chapter 19: How to Align the Logical and Emotional Sphere

Here it is, the secular battle between logic and emotion. A struggle between two opposite extremes. It's like when they want us to choose between what our heart wants and what our brain suggests us.

However, the truth is that if we pay more attention to this phenomenon, we'll easily realize that this opposition, this antithesis between brain and heart, doesn't have solid foundations.

It seems like a preconceived opposition, which formed from a linguistic or behavioral paradox, happened who knows how many centuries ago, and since then, someone has perpetuated it until it became a **rule**.

The rule of the heart always struggling with the hearth.

You know, it's common for two extremes to exert a certain seduction on the human mind, because human minds love challenges, and they love even more to **side** with one part, to witness its triumph.

This attitude is purely dictated by the sense of **competition**.

But competition doesn't favor happiness. On the contrary, we'd say that it contributes to the dispersion of happiness.

Do you know when true happiness exists?

It exists when you don't want to win anymore, because empathy with the loser is so strong that it prevents you from being happy for your victory.

Wise happiness exists when one doesn't want to win anymore, because one doesn't want to dominate over someone.

Wise happiness exists when you want to win only on the condition that you win all together. And that no one has to suffer defeat anymore.

It's about a certain level of wisdom, almost unthinkable for the current human mind.

And yet I bet that right now it seems reasonable to get this kind of happiness.

I bet you thought: could this be true?

And not: isn't this delusional?

If so, I can tell you that this faded recognition of truth testifies something very important: there's the seed of wisdom in you.

What seems inconceivable to you for your current thought patterns, it's not excluded that it can't also resonate as logical. If something inconceivable is more reasonable than delusional, it means that the inconceivable is only waiting to be made conceivable.

But how difficult it is to enter into the logic of the inconceivable!

Doesn't this seem to have a connection to the irremediable gap between logic and emotion?

If while you're thinking the thought of an apparent delusion you also feel that something resonates with you as logical, then it means that there has just been a co-presence of logic and emotion, a meeting or clash of logic and emotion.

A little barrier has just been destroyed.

Observe yourself while this barrier is being destroyed.

What's going on while you're feeling an emotion while you try to analyze something logically?

Is it possible that you feel a sort of inner peace, or something like that?

They've often been handed categorical information. An example? That poetry is not compatible with logic.

These people didn't evidently know the structure, content and function of riddles.

Riddles are games of logic.

And they were at best written in poetic form.

Therefore, there's a form of **poetry** with a logic **function**.

Hence, a riddle is the perfect model that guarantees cohesion between poetry and logic, without any battle or conflict.

Just a common goal: building the conditions for a game.

Does it seem weird that poetry unifies with logic because of a game?

It's not that weird, believe me.

There are people who claim that all existence is a game: the already omniscient consciousness gets fed up with its omniscience and relegates itself to a limited body, just for the sake of re-conquering the unlimited.

A game, indeed. A game that the consciousness chooses, maybe to escape the static state of omniscience.

But well, if we say that the entire existence is a game, then it's clear that even in the whole existence logic and poetry can coexist, just like it happens for logic and poetry in riddles.

Existence would be an enlarged and amplifies version of a riddle.

Who's stopping you from thinking it that way?

After all, when it comes to this life, we can't do anything but trying to guess!

We're always trying to guess the right choice to make, the right path to follow, the right person to meet. We're always trying to guess what's wrong or right, even before starting the process of understanding.

Before we try to understand something with the tools of conceptual thinking, we have this habit of guessing while we are still in the stage of preconceptual thinking.

Why do we even do this? Maybe it's a cultural legacy that we now carry around as a genetic code, that we inherited from our ancestors, whose knowledge included divination, or the art of guessing.

Whatever the source, we can't help but noticing logic and emotion are never disjointed a priori.

Even the emotion itself has its own inner logic!

And if we don't get to understand what's the logic of the emotion, it's certainly one of our limits, it's not about a conflict between logic and emotion!

Why do we tend to see a conflictual relationship where we simply can't catch an immediate relation?

The inner logic of emotion could be the same modulation of the emotion itself, the degree of minimum and maximum intensity, the threshold that allows the body to endure an emotion without risking to die from it. A self-modulation.

Please try not to trust that way of saying that always pit "brain against heart" and "logic against emotion": the brain and the heart, viewed holistically, are a whole, and their harmony is conducive to the harmony of the organism. Similarly, logic and emotion, viewed from a higher perspective, are portions of the existence that, when in harmony, harmonize existence itself.

Any thought that establishes the conflict as the fulfillment of two natural elements is a counterproductive thought:

The fulfillment is not the struggle between brain and heart, it's not the battle between emotion and logic, but it's the harmony between the parts, which we have temporarily lost.

Chapter 20: What Is and How Do We Improve Emotional Intelligence

- Emotional intelligence at work

- Emotional leadership

- Emotional intelligence for couples

- Emotional intelligence to win the right person

Once, out of curiosity, I wanted to interview a boy who had a 190-IQ. I was curious about his interests, but above all I was interested in observing and studying the speed at which he processed the information I proposed to him and the way he processed it. I wanted to understand, in short, how far he was from all the other people I had interviewed during my life, who had an average IQ.

Well, you won't believe the wave of sympathy that grabbed me when the interview came to an end.

The boy, whom we'll call Henri, greeted me with a grin of suspicion, as if wary of my role.

His first statement struck me deeply. He said, hey, we both know you don't give a damn about me. You're just here to study me. I am your lab rat.

He was easy-going, not at all embarrassed by my presence, which was actually irritating, at times annoying. So, I asked myself: what is keeping him here? Why did he agree to be interviewed?

I didn't say anything, because I wanted him to get everything out of his system. And then because, I have to admit, for the first time I was guilty of being curious. I was fascinated by that boy because we had something in common, he just didn't know it. And I let him think that he was just an experiment to me and that I was yet another experimenter. And that that conversation was yet another macabre workshop masquerading as a polite formality.

- How are you?

This was all I asked. Nothing more.

He looked at me with renewed eyes. The look of suspicion left space to a sort of bewilderment.

- Do you want to imprint my gestures in your mind, the unconscious gestures I make while I say that yes, I'm fine or that no, I'm not good at all? That no, I'm not good at all! Do you want to write down on some mnemonic sheet of paper my facial expressions?

It left me stunned to detect that repetition when he said twice: *no, I'm not good at all*. The first time it seemed like an illustrative answer, the second time it seemed to have become a heartfelt response.

- Is there anything I can do to help?

Again, the same bewilderment in his eyes, enhanced. Then he continued to speak.

- I haven't given you an answer yet. Why would you want to help me?

- I would still help you, even if you told me you were okay now. I would help you remember this moment better, maybe using some strategic words to imprint it in your memory, so you would fish this serenity out of the archives in times of sadness.

- So, let's recap. You're not here to imprint my gestures on your memory, but you're here to help me imprint my serenity on my memory? Oh, this is insane.

The boy looked down.

- This is really crazy. I love this interview!

- Well, have I increased your serenity a bit?

The boy flashed me a smile, his lips not yet parted, as if to protect himself.

- You think little geniuses are automatically happy, don't you?

- I don't, kid. I don't.

- Well, you're right. You're right not to believe that.

- Do you want to talk about it?

The boy let out a sigh that was somewhere between bewilderment and resignation at having to break for the umpteenth time the shell of words he did not intend to release. And yet, he probably felt a sense of guilt if he didn't release them.

- It's not true that I was born already facilitated in the working world. I started working as a child because I even worked to make my teachers understand me. They didn't understand my language; they struggled to follow me, they told me I was tortuous, that the ideas were there, but the words were never in the right place or in the right order. In truth, I could feel the disorder in their speeches. Eventually, it all became clear to me.

We simply had different ways of registering and channeling the semantics of words.

That boy expressed himself in a hypnotic way, but perhaps he didn't even notice it, so used to his style in linguistic coherence with his usual flow of thought.

- And then when the newspapers say that people like me are born brilliant, they never say that the recognition of this brilliance comes later, or maybe never comes. That being born brilliant doesn't mean growing up brilliant, being born a certain way doesn't mean growing up a certain way. At school, no one ever congratulated me because they thought I was brilliant. I was faster at finding the solution to certain problems, and the only thing I remember is that at those times they looked at me like I was an alien. It's not like they were saying, wow, thank you, you just solved a problem for us! Actually, in those moments, a problem was subtracted, and a problem was added. And the new problem had every appearance of being my presence.

- Are you saying that your above average IQ has never made you feel luckier than average?

- If genetics were sentient, would I thank it for endowing me with such an IQ? No. Would I curse it? Not even. Basically, I can tell you that I don't feel lucky or even unlucky. But, lo and behold, I have sometimes dreamed of being like them... Not superior... Just like everyone else...

The boy instantly noticed that my eyes were getting progressively shiny as I tried to keep them sheltered with the dark frames of my prescription glasses. He didn't say anything. He simply stopped talking for a while. Maybe he was waiting for me to say something.

But that didn't happen.

He spoke to me.

- This instead, yours, I mean, must be emotional intelligence.

Dear reader, I just showed you that a high IQ doesn't qualify your future, and it doesn't decide in advance the possibilities you'll have in your life. It doesn't make you a lucky person. More importantly: it doesn't make you a happy person. I've shown you how you can be deeply intelligent and deeply discouraged.

Perhaps, however, the ending of this short story can introduce the topic I want to talk about now.

Emotional intelligence.

First of all, let's explain what emotional intelligence is.

Emotional intelligence is the ability to orient, comprehend, functionally manage one's own emotions and others' emotions. It's the ability to distinguish an emotion from any other one and to use this faculty of distinction to be able to move better on the plane of actions and thoughts.

And that's not everything.

Emotional intelligence is what allows us to express, analyze, intuit a certain emotion. It's the ability to create feelings whenever they're needed for the proper functioning of thoughts. It's the ability to use the same emotions to favor intellectual (and emotional) growth.

You see, emotional intelligence is many, many things!

It has been defined in several ways over time.

In psychology it's now established that emotional intelligence favors **self-efficacy**.

What does it mean to enhance self-efficacy?

It means possessing a good dose of emotional intelligence constitutes a real added value to your existence! This type of intelligence can improve your own existence and increase the ability to shape events that threaten it.

In fact, it has been studied that emotional intelligence contributes to the development of **problem-solving** skills, other than favoring the communicative exchange with other individuals, and therefore, give birth to a constructive thinking.

Think about it: isn't it by getting into the emotions of others that you can have smoother communication?

The better one succeeds to enter someone's emotion, the better you can communicate with that someone.

Because when we have a clear idea in mind of what the emotion of our interlocutor is, we know exactly **what to say and what not to say** to modify that type of emotion to direct it in other ways, or simply not to be misunderstood.

 Suppose we have to deal with a very touchy person. Well, if we learn how to deal with his inner book of emotions, we know how to identify the moments in which it's better to speak or keep quiet to avoid triggering negative emotions, which in the end will only lead to quarrels and fights.

Suppose we have to deal with someone who believes everything one says too easily. If we learn to read the book of his emotions, we'll know when the moment to stop comes, because if we keep on joking, it's possible that that person takes too seriously our narration of events and ends up believing what we're saying.

And now, starting from these two examples, let's move into the field of employment.

Can emotional intelligence be useful in our job?

Sure it can!

Imagine you have to make a good impression on your employee. If you manage to catch easily, promptly, and effectively his emotions, you'll intuitively understand what he's looking for in a person and what qualities will impress him.

Can it improve your efficiency?

Yes, without a doubt. Emotional intelligence, even being an ability that allows us to program and orient one's own emotions, can also help us when a negative emotion wants to prevail during an important job commitment.

For example, if we're working on an urgent project and we're invaded by a sense of sudden fear, thanks to emotional intelligence we'll be able to analyze and evaluate the reason: once it will be understood, it will be easier to eliminate it.

This ability to manage the intensity, time and manner of your emotions automatically succeeds in increasing your self-esteem. Because the moment you manage to "unravel" one of your emotional movements, you also feel more motivated in your job.

In short: you realize that you have managed to understand a mechanism that was limiting your performance, and by understanding it, you'll manage to eliminate it.

So, your work can pick up where it left off, without those annoying obstacles and unforeseen hiccups that often take the form of emotions.

This realization will certainly make you very satisfied, don't you think?

The elimination of negative emotion generates a positive emotion.

This positive emotion you'll conquer for yourself is going to enrich the baggage of your emotional experiences.

And this enrichment will be another victory for your emotional intelligence.

This type of intelligence is very flexible: it can improve and strengthen itself throughout our whole lives.

It's a type of non-dictatorial intelligence, because it doesn't impose its standard: you're the one who gets to decide **when and how** to potentiate it.

Emotional intelligence will be there, still, just waiting for your signal to start working in the ways that are most useful to you.

Work efficiency is particularly connected to emotional intelligence. Another example?

Embarrassment –

You're working on a marketing project, and you're tasked with choosing the perfect headline to grab the attention of your audience. If your emotional intelligence is particularly well developed, you won't have much difficulty finding the perfect headline. It's precisely emotional intelligence that tells you the best way to appeal to the emotions of others.

When you're aware of the mechanisms that govern your emotions and the emotions of others, I assure you that all it takes is a little practice with words, and a web of words can move a web of emotions.

This is how you can practice with word combinations, if you can gain a more extensive knowledge of the language by being able to pick up and memorize keywords, you'll be absolutely perfect when you need to choose the right words to catch the public's attention.

Wittgenstein, a very interesting philosopher, once wrote: "The limits of my language are the limits of my world."

Emotional intelligence always grows together with the enrichment of the language: the emotion communicated to the outside needs a tool: **words**.

The more words you'll know, the more communications you'll be able to express, the more emotions you'll manage to move through the use of words.

Words don't just have the role of communicating your emotions to the external world, but they also have the role of activating and moving others' emotions.

Which are the benefits of emotional leadership?

Emotional intelligence is fundamental to get a good performance in emotional leadership.

But what's exactly emotional leadership?

We can briefly say that it's about a functional approach for the management of a certain environment, in a particular way in the working environment. This approach is based on the ability to promote and manage the emotional components at their best in the group.

For example, if you have to carry out a project, and you will be the emotional leader of the group, you will know exactly how to increase the **motivational** tone of the project participants. With emotional intelligence you can, in fact, help the members of the group to discover, develop and enhance talents, both expressed and unexpressed, and to unleash latent skills. A good emotional leader knows how to recognize and sniff out even an unexpressed talent or latent ability, because he or she can read the symptoms that indicate the presence of a certain quality. For example, a very persuasive way of speaking may indicate a philosopher's skill; or always being able to find the right words to express a concept may indicate a writer's skill. However, to be able to grasp these details, the leader must be equipped with a lot of emotional intelligence. Because this information does not always come spontaneously to attention; on the contrary, sometimes it needs a correspondence of intentions, empathy and identification.

Understanding others' emotions is the key that will lead any of your project to unimaginable success.

Understanding other's emotions also means to **collocate**. This means you'll know **where** to collocate the members of the project. I mean, it means that if you recognize their talents and abilities, you can find the right place for them, and thus make the final result more brilliant.

Understanding others' emotions also means **cohesion**.

Imagine succeeding at immediately catch, with the adequate readiness, the discomforts of the whole group.

What comes out of it?

The result is a valorization of social **cohesion** within the group. And experience teaches us that when cohesion is good, also the prediction of success is good. The classic tight-knit group that works better is no legend to keep only for childish fairy tales.

Have you ever felt to do something better after you had a nice sleep?

A restful sleep certainly produces physical wellness. It's clear. And physical wellness, just like emotional wellness, disposes of the conditions to perform at your full potential.

Relational wellness among the members is expressed in an improvement of the job performance.

At any rate, one should also focus on the possible disadvantages of emotional leadership.

In fact, when it isn't well balanced, one risks plumbing into a series of complications that might even slow down success or even determine failure.

For example, emotions could contaminate the neutral vision of an action or could lead to impulsive reactions, which would turn out to be unbecoming.

But don't be afraid: these complications **only** take place if you can't handle balancing emotional intelligence, measuring it with other aspects to keep in mind.

Now I'll try to show you some strategies to better handle the control of this emotional balance.

1) **Understand emotions keeping the right emotional detachment.** That is: when you identify with a certain emotional movement, be agile enough to be able to get out of it completely. Many times, people get stuck in the identification, even with just a little piece of mind, with the risk of compromising themselves.

2) **Don't lose the objective of sight, even when you feel overwhelmed.** Another mistake in the management of emotions is that it's very easy to be carried away by them, tipping the scale too much on their favor, at the expense of logical planning. This can lead to the loss of sight of the final goal. But if you know how to keep it firm, fixed in your mind and if you – even when you'll be busy thinking about something else – will know how to be constantly concentrated on it, I assure you that this objective won't slip out of your mind. This journey could beneficiate from meditation and visual creativity techniques, during which you should train to project yourself in the scenario of your goal.

3) **Try to look at the emotion with renewed eyes.** You'll simply have to break free from the idea you've always had about emotions. The emotion, this time, has to become purely **functional** and stop being **recreational**. If you need a certain emotion to achieve the desired result, then keep it. If it's not useful, try to get rid of it as soon as you can. In daily life situations we're used to carrying with us all the emotions we feel, as if they were an inner bag, and this is how we carry their load wherever we go. Well:

keep in mind that this mustn't happen in your job. Useless emotions could slow down the project at hand.

Emotional Intelligence for couples.

How would you react if I told you that what determines a break up is not the conflict per se, but the inexact communication of that conflict?

Please, don't take this rhetorical question too seriously.

Many times, we witness the end of long love stories because of a very small, almost ridiculous conflict, compared to the intensity of that love.

But then, what's the real conflict of that separation?

If the **disproportion** between the dimension of the conflict and the dimension of love is so evident, is it possible that there's a third element that determined that separation?

Yes. I propose the presence of this suffused third element.

And I underline suffused, because it's almost invisible, like an impersonal current flowing within the conflict and never reveals itself, except in its effects.

This third element, which has the shape of a current, is called **incommunicability**.

And incommunicability is the first engine of **misunderstanding**.

And if you add conflict to the incommunicability and misunderstanding, here's what you got: a huge problem.

And this is where the real source of the separation, perhaps, lies.

In the imprecise interweaving of an absolute incomprehension. And where does this incomprehension come from?

Well, from **the impossibility to communicate their emotions to each other.**

It's not always a problem strictly related to words! Many times, the problem lies in the root of language, that is, it lies in the world of meanings and not in the world of the words they can be translated with.

In the world of meanings lie emotional meanings.

Well. Let's now suppose that a couple, endowed with poor emotional intelligence, quarrels because of the wrong transfer of a word, and that is because of a misunderstanding of a speech.

A way to make this up is to **trace back the origin of the emotion that produced that type of word.**

But the couple, indeed endowed with poor emotional intelligence, hasn't got the ability to do so and therefore gets stuck, entrenched, in this cage of misunderstanding because of a wrong word. With the result that, that quarrel will **always** remain **unresolved** for who knows for how long, because the root cause had never been untangled.

Now, let's try to imagine the same situation with a couple endowed with a higher emotional intelligence. What would have happened?

Probably, the couple wouldn't take long to find the "**source that caused that misunderstood word**," and once the reason for the emotion was clarified, everything would have ended up well.

There's no wrong word that can't be repaired by a right emotion.

And this is why emotional intelligence comes to the rescue of the couple, as if it was a wonderful repairer of things impossible to repair.

One can't say there are irreparable fights, at least until we get to the source of the emotion from which the quarrels arose.

And if the emotion can confirm the inevitability of the quarrel, it's true that it can also disprove it.

Anyway, whatever the reason to use emotional intelligence, one can be sure of something: it will always guide you in the right direction.

Because if the quarrel is also confirmed by its emotional root, it means that those two persons are incompatible.

If instead the quarrel gets disproved by its emotional root, it means that those two persons are compatible, but **they don't know they are**.

Isn't the power of emotional intelligence wonderful?

And how painful it is to think of the couples that ended, exploded, just like that, in a bubble of air that could have simply been sucked out by the clarity of an emotion.

Who knows how many things believed destroyed could have been rebuilt, thanks to emotional intelligence?

Who knows how many things believed to be dead could have been revived, thanks to emotional intelligence?

So, what are you waiting for?

You need to start right now boosting your emotional intelligence! The stakes are too high to pass up such an opportunity.

Below are some methods to boost your emotional intelligence.

1) Imagine others' emotional experiences.

Here's a typical situation. You're on Facebook, and you suddenly read a brutal, offensive, humiliating comment directed to a celebrity.

Your immediate reaction is to feel disgusted for the author of that comment. But... what if I told you that you can overcome the phase of disgust to get to a deeper comprehension?

We often stop to this thought: "damn, how is it possible for a person to say something like that? I could never do that!"

In short, we stop at the phase in which we realize to be **detached** from that condemnable behavior.

But what if, after this detachment, we tried to get closer?

I know it seems absurd and maybe also mean. I know you wish you never got close to someone like that.

But you see, monsters get tamed only when they're closely studied.

All you have to do is this: imagine the reasons that determined the choice of that comment. If the comment is humiliating, you ask yourself: what satisfaction could he get from humiliating? Is it possible that he, too, was humiliated as a child?

And so now he wants to imitate his tormentors? Or is it pure sadism?

And what if he wants to be seen, to be recognized, even if in the most despicable way, because throughout his life he has been unheard, and he has learned that only with words that displace him he stops being ignored?

Warning: this analysis should not lead you to empathize with the guilty party and justify him.

It simply must lead you to understand a spectrum of emotional possibilities that led to those words.

2) Identify in others' emotional moment.

Every time you witness someone's emotion, be it just someone you know or a complete strange, try to feel what he feels in that exact moment.

This is a very useful exercise to **cross** others' emotional domain.

When you cross the other's emotion, somehow that emotion will show up to you in all its shades, in a new perspective, that you were missing before. Because one single emotion can be felt in millions of different ways by millions of different human beings.

And so? And so, you'll be dealing with the completeness of an emotion. An incomplete emotion that is viewed from a multiple perspective becomes, as it goes, a complete emotion.

If someone is happy for a success, a healing, even for a beautiful dream, observe him in the smallest details, in the micro-movements of the eyes, in the expression of the face, in the modulation of the voice. Strive in this way to trace the origin of those movements, that expression and that modulation.

Do the same thing with sadness. If someone is sad about a failure, an illness, even a nightmare, observe them closely, and repeat the same process. Do you know what the most striking note is? That when you try to comfort them, you'll feel like you're comforting yourself. And you'll see, you'll see that your comfort for that person will be absolutely better than it has ever been before.

In your sole effort to **interpret**, you'll already be doing a great job of **understanding**.

Even if it is not immediately clear to you at that moment that you have gone through its emotional wringer, one-day opportunities will arise again that will show you the results of your effort.

What if I told you that emotional intelligence can even be useful in winning over the right person?

That's it. It's a very likely assumption, and you shouldn't be so skeptical about it. I'll try to explain you why.

Think about it: to win someone's heart, it's necessary to understand which are the things that catch that someone's attention. And how can we do that, if not through an attentive emotional evaluation?

I'll explain myself better. If the person you like is irremediably attracted, for example, by very acculturated people, you can get to intuit that very soon, thanks to emotional intelligence.

In fact, you'll observe with reasonable astuteness the behaviors that person has every time he approaches an acculturated subject.

But apart from this, and more in general, you'll get to observe how his behavior changes in relation to everything else.

And from that apparently simple observation, the more your emotional intelligence is developed, the sooner you will be able to draw the sums of his or her preferences.

Any change his face produces, any change in the tone of voice, gestures, etc., if you'll get him well framed within a mental scheme of yours, it will be the light guiding your path to his heart.

Yes, winning the right person begins with the understating of the emotivity that characterizes that person.

Don't worry. He won't even notice you're studying him. Because your analysis will be compenetrated by neutrality. Emotional intelligence works mainly in an occult and subliminal way. Sometimes, indeed, almost always, emotional intelligence works without you even noticing it... let alone if an outsider will notice it! There is no danger!

I just wish you could understand first that emotional intelligence before being useful to win the right person is useful to make you understand the prototype of your right person. Therefore, emotional intelligence plays on a dual background: on one side, it protects you from the misunderstanding of your sentimental needs, on the other one it makes you understand what the other person's needs are. We could say you're safe even from yourself, that is, you're safe for your own misjudgments.

How many times have you mulled over the possible tastes of the person you like? I bet you've done this many times, so now you could really use a little voice from within to strategically suggest what moves to make and what moves to avoid in order to be in tune with the sentimental search of the person you like.

You see, emotional intelligence allows you to pick up on those details that signal the presence of attention and focus on certain things. For example, if the person you like starts looking fascinated when he hears the news on the local radio, thanks to emotional intelligence you will be able to distinctly guess which object of the speech dictated by the radio has captured his attention, even arousing a feeling of sudden fascination. Each reaction is linked to particular movements that are not missed by those who train by studying the movements of human beings.

In fact, **if you start studying the way all human beings' emotions work,** you will then be able to easily detect the emotions that characterize a single human being, because it will be enough to isolate him from the context of the study while preserving the notional basis of the study.

Yes, you get my point perfectly. In order to potentiate emotional intelligence, it's important that you study a good psychology book dedicated to the contextual manifestation of human emotions. Clearly studying alone is not enough, because it will have to be integrated with your assumptions, your additional reasoning, added to what you study. By integrating notional study with personal life experience, you will obtain remarkable and functional results.

Like any other sphere in life, the integration of two factors leads to the solution.

Think about it: for years, developmental psychology has been marked by debates between theories that privileged the role of nature and the ones who privileged the role of culture. And in the end?

In the end, they realized that the most convincing result should have come from an **integration** of **both nature and culture.**

History teaches us that separation is a source of error. History teaches us that the connection among elements repairs errors.

What could possibly potentiate emotional intelligence?

For sure, something that involves a **connection** and not a **separation**. You don't have to think about emotional intelligence as a more or less big split of absolute intelligence.

These assumptions given: I trust your enormous capacity to use your inner potentialities.

These are the fundamentals ingredients: theoretical study and experience in the field.

Emotional intelligence, other than allowing you to be more receptive in the recognition of **the right person for you**, also helps you detecting the **field of wrong people**.

You must imagine yourself as if you had two invisible antennae able to pick up the signals of someone who's going to hurt you. It would be a dream, wouldn't it?

You could save a huge waste of time!

And who knows how many people stole precious time from you. The time you could have spent much better!

Hey, get ready to say goodbye to this vicious circle made of mistakes of evaluation.

No wrong person is going to mask so good to prevent you from seeing his danger. You'll exactly know how to pick up the danger signals, even under the dual, more sophisticated, more mimetic mask.

You won't allow anyone to invade your time and space, your system of thought, your emotional stability, without your permission.

And thanks to emotional intelligence – trust me! – you won't ever be fooled by verbal flatteries, apparently innocence, a previously thought double game, a toxic character. Or anyway, the margin of error will be very, very, very reduced compared to what it used to be before.

Don't waste any more time. Get involved in the study and exercises and experiment the innumerable advantages of this type of intelligence.

Chapter 21: Learning How to Know Oneself to Understand Where Emotions Come From

Don't forget this: to understand where emotions come from, you'll have to learn to know yourself. Can you tell yourself you know yourself?

Can you tell yourself you have at least tried to get to know yourself?

You've often thought about it, I know. But there was probably no time, or you convinced yourself that there was no time. Introspective, self-reflective, meta-cognitive research, I mean, the inner research, scares us terribly when we're not ready to find out that we won't like what we're going to find there.

But you see, there's a moment in which it's important to accept that we're not impeccable, indeed sometimes it would be good to exaggerate and even imagine ourselves capable of being and thinking about something low and reprehensible. There's a nature that escapes the vigil consciousness, it's a corrupted, tainted nature that we can educate, and that – however – belongs to us.

This is why we shouldn't get scared if we ever found visible traces of this nature within ourselves. What we have inside doesn't define us, because we have the power to change, modify, file down the impulses until they become harmless enough to allow us to live a civil coexistence. But we can't ignore the fact that our animal heritage made us inherit Unseemly instincts. The real self-knowledge starts by accepting the animal counterpart to sublimate. If there's a negative feeling inside of you that you can't explain to yourself, it's probably a feeling that doesn't belong to you, and it's something pre-set that you absolutely have to eliminate in order to avoid clashes with your real personality.

Inner conflict comes from the recognition of a destructive or self-destructive tendency inside of us that could have a faster resolution if one only knew that it's important not to identify totally with everything that crosses our psyche.

Don't forget that our psyche is also crossed by fake memories and therefore is able to create scenes that don't belong to us, and can certainly create tendencies and behaviors that are not ours.

Thus, knowing oneself means exactly to discern what's invented by our dreamy, disconnected psyche, carried by unconscious imitations of all the behaviors that other people have or had with you.

Have you ever thought about this?

Maybe some incongruities you perceive inside of you are simply automatic imitations of people's eyesores, that is, unconscious imitations, staged by a naïve area of your psyche, still childish, that doesn't discern between good and bad, that doesn't know how to distinguish and therefore imitates everything it gets to observe and listen.

Instead, where do your emotions come from?

First of all, you have to understand that emotions can either be spontaneous or machinic. In fact, they can arise from learning by imitations that now translates into non-felt emotions, which automatically start just out of habit.

Fear, for example.

How many times did it happen to you to feel **unmotivated fear**?

There were no reasons to justify it, and yet it presented itself regularly.

Well, where does it come from? Is it really **yours**?

Not always. You see, we're going back to what we said before on behaviors that are imitated by the psyche; here, imagine a similar process, valid also for emotions.

What would happen?

You'd project someone's fear inside of yourself, and you'd think it's one of your remote fears!

Wouldn't that be terrible?

I mean, spending the rest of your life trembling because of others' fears, being afraid because of their fears.

Well, I don't want you to find yourself unprepared for such a situation. Start digging inside of yourself. Now.

Don't get distracted by the embarrassment of what you might find or by the fear of clashing with some terrible memory. Remember: you're going back in time just to move better ahead in time.

Come on! Fish out all of your fears. From the first one that comes to your mind to the last one you've felt, to the one that made you jerk, or feel a weight on your chest, or that made you tighten a knot in your throat.

Now take them, grab them, one by one.

Contextualize them.

Fill them with whys, fill them with how and when.

But most importantly, fill them with true or false, fill them with questions, fill them with this question: are you mine, or aren't you?

And now ask yourself if that fear, the one you never got to understand, that one which you can't really explain to yourself, and there you go: ask yourself if it belongs to your parents or a sibling, to a friend, a past lover, or the protagonist of a movie.

What has your irrational mind done?

It feared something that belonged to someone else and made you think it was yours.

Talk to it. Talk to your irrational mind.

You're facing each other now.

Tell it: I'm sorry, I will no longer believe this. I will no longer believe you. Tell it: **these fears were never mine, and now I free myself from them, because what's not mine should be returned.**

At the end of this exercise of restitution, understanding of your own emotions and of purification from the non-authentic ones, you could feel a dizziness, a sense of alienation from yourself, of imbalance, disorder or lurch.

Well, if you have such a symptom, it means that the process of liberation of false fears is working.

The symptom shows it's working.

Instead, if there's no symptom: don't worry. There are people who can get to purify themselves passively because perhaps their unconscious decided not to manifest the symptom to the unconscious.

But this doesn't mean that your unconscious isn't feeling a dizziness: let's just say that you're not allowed to feel it.

Does it even matter, after all?

What matters is that you get out of this page conscious of having uprooted a chain of deception.

It may seem far-fetched to you, and maybe you're thinking: how can such a short page cope with such a long chain of fears?

I suggest you don't underestimate the power of a sparking: it can start a fire.

Chapter 22: How to Use the Jedi Method to Master Your Inner Self

The Jedi master of *Star Wars* has left a legacy of precious teachings for mastering our inner Self and become leaders of ourselves: the best versions of leaders we've always wanted to be.

1) Unlearn everything you've learned.

Maybe you're wondering: what? And why did I have to learn them anyway?

Actually, it doesn't make any sense, as long as the question is exhausted this way. Because the exact sense lies in the next step.

It's not about **learning to unlearn**, but it's about **unlearning to learn better**.

When you think you've learned something, that something often turns into a certainty, a conviction. Do you know what the terrible vice of convictions is? That they make the thought immobile.

The engine of thoughts, what makes them move, is the **doubt**.

Without any doubt, there's just static. And where there's static, the intellect petrifies itself.

Thus, you'll get that unlearning means inserting the doubt again in a database of certainties. By triggering the presence of doubt, everything will start to move again, and when the movement shows up again, you'll feel renewed in intellect.

Isn't it the continuous renewal that makes things evolve? Think about it: the cells of our body regenerates continuously. If we become immobile with our certainties, it's difficult to get the renewal of the thought, and therefore its consequential evolution.

And it's not everything. Thanks to your new cognitive tools naturally acquired during time, all the information learned previously (once it's unlearnt) can be re-learned in a better way, because your cognitive ability, which presides over the processing, is now perfected.

Have you ever tried? Have you ever tried to re-watch a cartoon you used to watch as a child and realize to understand its overall meaning? Not even this: let's go further.

More than the cartoon itself, you feel like you understand the exact intention of the creator.

It is no longer an aggregate of enchanting shapes and colors that entertained your childhood attention.

Today, that cartoon speaks to you about everyone's childhood, not just your own childhood; it tells you about the processes that characterize children's preferences.

And you feel as if you are immersing yourself in the psyche of everyone else, in the emotions of all the children who were not you.

Isn't this a manifestation of all human emotional intelligence we were talking about? Here it is. Also, this is an exercise to potentiate it. To participate emotionally to the mechanism of attention and of other ones, even feeling part of a group of people who had the same experience of watching the same cartoon. And you ask yourself: who knows if the other ones, during this scene, felt some hostility towards the teacher, or here we have this other scene, who knows if they felt compassionate for the figure of the girl, and going on, a sense of resentment for the figure of the girl's friend, who was prettier.

How many unexplored worlds can you explore when you unlearn something old?

2) We are the fertile soil that sees the birth of his disciples.

Don't forget this: whatever you do, even the most mundane thing, will have an impact on someone else.

Maybe you can argue: okay, but if for example today I'm wearing a blue coat instead of wearing a black one, what impact could I possibly have on the other person?

Here, try to picture this scene in your mind.

You have just arrived at the station and are waiting for the subway to arrive, with your blue coat neatly laid out. A woman, from a distance, unintentionally begins to stare at you, caught by the particular color you are wearing. While staring at you, the woman accidentally collides with a stranger. He says to her, "Ma'am, forgive me, are you hurt?" She tells him, "No, you forgive me, I always have my head in the clouds." The stranger looks at her. He has a lightning strike. She looks at him. And she thinks that all that thoughtfulness had never been given to her by anyone before that moment.

Eventually, the two go out for a drink together.

See, your blue coat, determining the woman's accident, was the driving force behind the date!

What you did had an impact on two people.

But now, let's go back to where we were before, in your first-person experience.

You look at your watch. It's getting late. You keep on waiting for the subway to arrive, you still have your blue coat on.

A man is sitting on a station bench.

At one point, his gaze stops on the color of your coat. The man has an advertising catalog in his hands, and he's flipping through the winter coat section. He has to buy a new coat and is unsure about the color to choose.

Looking at the color harmony that is created between your hair color and the blue of your coat, the man (who has the same hair color as you) has no doubt: he will opt for a beautiful blue coat.

When he comes back home, he stops at the catalog store. He buys the blue coat he had seen on the paper, preferring it to a gray coat that cost twenty dollars more.

And guess what?

With the money left over, he was able to donate it to three beggars who had settled in the vicinity of the store.

Well, again, I give you my compliments. Your blue coat contributed to charity!

Now can you see what I mean when I say that everything you do has an impact on others? Whether you want it to or not, whether you are aware of it or not. Directly or indirectly. It just happens.

If even the choice of the color of a coat can influence the course of other people's lives, can you imagine how much your behavior, the way you carry yourself, the way you interact, the way you speak can influence others' lives?

Hence, try to always keep it in mind.

If the leader is a fertile field, the leader also has the responsibility to work on himself, he has the responsibility to stay tuned, to perfect himself and improve not only for himself but also for his future disciples.

    3) Learning to detach from what one's afraid to lose.

If you're afraid of losing something, perhaps it doesn't really belong to you.

In fact, how could you lose something that's impressed on you as if it was a genetic trait?

Maybe, if you lose the object that qualifies it, you lose the memory of the name that it defines, but if the print of its breath really touched you inside, you can never really lose it.

Then, you are afraid of losing things that could get lost.

But things that can get lost aren't that important, after all.

What matters is just what's eternal: what doesn't die, and therefore, even before not-dying for itself, it doesn't die for you as well.

So please, stop being afraid of losing things that, because of their nature, can be lost.

Where nature disposes the possibility of getting lost, it means that that something doesn't have a great value for your evolution.

Don't be distracted by ephemeral things, things that come and go. Or at least, yes, let let them go, but don't allow them to determine your fear. Alright?

Fear is a too toxic feeling to be triggered by ephemeral executioners. Fear is no match for what produces it.

Why would an object that can be broken and lost trigger fear in me?

That item is worthless!

And instead, the symbolic meaning of that object is not broken or lost, because it's not contained in the object itself, but in your representation of it: therefore, it is within you.

The object dies, the symbol knows no boundaries.

The symbol is inside you. You decide.

You decide the fate of the symbol.

When you introject the things of the world, you feed yourself with the true meaning of objects. You don't own an object when you manipulate it, but when you understand the mechanism that allows you to manipulate it.

So what? You'll have to detach yourself with your mind and soul from the things you're afraid of losing.

I assure you that this detachment will grant you an inner serenity that you probably don't even expect.

You must possess the idea of an object, and not the object itself; the idea of a person, and not the person itself.

And can you lose the idea of an object or the idea of a person? No. Ideas don't get lost.

They are not lost, not even if one day your brain succumbs to the diseases of old age. Ideas are not even lost when a brain disease prevents you from communicating them to others: ideas remain within you, perhaps especially when you are unable to express them.

Because at that precise moment, at that very moment, you'll be alone with your ideas. You'll be alone with the most precious things you possess.

Chapter 23: Theories and Practices to Win Resentment, Performance Anxiety, Fear, Procrastination, and jealousy

Do you know what fills the soul with toxins?

Resentment.

I ask you to interrogate yourself. Yes, right now, in the exact moment you're reading my words.

Do you feel resentment for anyone?

If the answer is yes, I want to warn you right away: you have to get rid of it, like, right now.

Every process of inner purification can't be separated from a liberation of resentment.

Even if you never think about it, I assure you that resentment keeps on acting without you knowing it, until it lives, until you allow it.

Resentment means "still feeling the painful effects of something," or maybe it means "irritation towards something or someone."

In both cases there are two highly poisonous components: pain and irritation.

When a wound causes pain, it requires medications. When a wound provokes irritation, it requires medications.

Both wounds ask for a solution.

So, can you get that resentment is a disposition to uproot, finding a solution?

If you feel resentment towards something or someone, I want to ask you to use your emotional intelligence.

Would you believe it if I told you that the more emotionally intelligent you are, the faster you will be able to get rid of any resentment?

I would like you to think about the person or people you resent.

But I wish you could think about this person – or people – in a special way.

I want you to try to rebuild the past of these people. Starting from infancy, up to the moment you were resented.

Can you imagine the reconstruction of their lives before they contributed to ruining yours?

What do you see?

You see, forgiving is not easy at all. But this is something we all know, it's not news.

Detaching from a painful event, however, doesn't mean forgiving: it simply means to **take away from the painful event the power to make you grieve.**

But in order to detach from the painful event, you also have to make **harmless** the person that caused it to you.

You know, I have an optimal method to make my tormentors harmless and get free from any resentment.

I imagine them in two versions: in their past and in their future versions.

I imagine them when they were infants, in a crib, children ignored by their parents, growing up in the midst of contempt, humiliation, lack of empathy, in the midst of a family that demanded more, always more, in a perpetual climate of competition with siblings, with cousins, with guests' children.

Then I imagine them elderly, abandoned in turn by the children they failed to raise to love, left like this to rot in a hospice, with a sagging heart, swollen ankles, and a ravaged brain repeating the words the child repeated.

Here: your executioners become poor human beings who have been and will be punished by life and do not need the punishment of your resentment.

And most importantly: **you don't need to be punished because of your resentment. Because resentment, in truth, is a punishment for yourself and not for those towards whom it is directed.**

Fear and performance anxiety: analysis of a fine line.

When you're about to get close to a goal, you happen to run into the performance anxiety phase.

It's time to understand why.

Performance anxiety dates to the education you received when you were a child. Parents often project on their children everything they ever wanted to realize in their own life and that they didn't manage to accomplish.

Parents see in their sons the fulfillment of their unexpressed ambition. In this regard, they insist on the damaging practice of demanding from their children what they have not been able to demand from themselves.

The result, visible especially in the long run, is the feeling of always having to meet the expectations of others, no matter whether those others are family members or perfect strangers.

The family setting has resulted in a likely mixture of the (healthy) sense of personal achievement and the (unhealthy) sense of conquering the expectations of others.

All this is reflected in the preparatory phase that anticipates a goal and results in the phenomenon of performance anxiety.

The same educational layer, however, can be observed in the phenomenon of fear. When a parent expects from the child the lack of self-realization, disguised as caring, it often happens that the child experiences the fear of not living up to expectations. So that the mechanism of fear, implicated in the mechanism of performance anxiety, has already been inaugurated by bad parenting, as you can see. Getting rid of parental patterns, going back to the roots, is a great way to get rid of performance anxiety and even fear.

Another unfortunate consequence of performance anxiety is called: **procrastination**.

How does procrastination emerge from performance anxiety?

Evidently, there's a tendency to procrastinate, to put off the goal further and further away, perhaps precisely to avoid the pre-operational phase that underlies performance anxiety.

In short, anxiety can be so violent that it can push someone to prefer to move away from the goal, because moving away can also carry performance anxiety away. So, people give up the time of success for fear of the anxiety that precedes success.

And again, it's important to go back to the triggers that have stabilized the anxiety component related to one's goals. It is necessary to break down the belief that every goal is systematically preceded by the phase of anxiety and fear: the moment you manage to see the positive of the goal, I doubt that procrastination will still be so present in your life.

Overcoming jealousy

To overcome jealousy, we must first understand what originates the feeling of jealousy. Jealousy is not a feeling that is produced in isolation and independently from other things, but always depends on a mental representation. And this mental representation is possession.

If I am afraid of someone else taking a loved one away from me, it means that I can't yet feel effective happiness for the happiness of the person I love. I mean... why do I believe that **someone** is taking the person away from me, and I don't believe that **person** is choosing to be taken away by someone?

Why do we believe that person belongs to us?

The sense of belonging is absolutely threatening, limiting, unfair, and an inevitable source of suffering.

When you are assailed by jealousy, try to keep these words in mind: there is no such thing as **my** friend, **my** partner, **my** family member. There is only one consciousness that has come to this planet to experience, and that is particularly attuned to my consciousness. But being in tune with my consciousness does not define that person as **belonging** to my consciousness. If I love this person, I must allow him or her to experience, to be enriched, even by other consciousnesses than myself!

When you overcome the barrier of a sense of belonging, you will be able to see jealousy as something completely unbecoming to yourself and others.

Chapter 24: Learn the Art of Detachment

What does one overcome first?

Detachment from a sense of belonging, or detachment from achievement?

Who knows if they're interconnected!

After all, in both cases… you'll have to give up feeling bad.

The real question is: **are you ready to be fine?**

Are you ready to stop feeling bad?

If your answer is yes, then I'll explain to you a method to learn how to be detached from the outcome.

It's about directing your motivations differently.

If, for example, you perform an action only by virtue of the outcome, you must anticipate to yourself that **you don't really like that action.**

And if you want to be happy, you shouldn't be doing something you don't like!

If, on the other hand, you perform an action by virtue of the satisfaction that the performance of that action brings you, then, tell me: **what do you care about the result? You really like that action, and you like it regardless of the result.**

So, whatever the result, you will be positively enriched by it, and the sense of satisfaction will certainly have preceded the result, because it has always been intrinsic to the action itself.

The art of detachment from the result isn't something monstrous that you learn after who knows how many years of practice! It's just a different orientation of your essential motivation.

When your motivation revolves around the action taken and not around its result, you will see that detachment will arise spontaneously, without you even going to look for it.

Chapter 25: 21 Days to Get to Master Your Emotions

Let's try to break down the final steps that will accompany your emotional milestone into three weeks.

First week.

1) Take some time to study, analyze and evaluate all the varieties of emotions that will emerge in you, in a wide variety of situations, from the most common to the most unusual.

2) Try to put each emotion into context. Observe the frequency with which a certain type of emotion is repeated in a certain type of context and try to draw a mental statistic. At the end of this exercise, you may be able to predict an emotion just by getting into the right context.

3) Determine which emotions are toxic to achieving your goals. Focus on eliminating toxic emotions through anticipating them. Try to understand the reasons that make you available to the toxic emotion: it's not about eliminating the emotion, because that's not possible, and anyone who tells you otherwise is lying to you. You don't have to eliminate the toxic emotion, but you have to make yourself no longer available to the toxic emotion. So that it continues to exist without being able to touch you.

Second week.

1) After studying the emotions that arise in you, it's your turn to study the emotions that arise in others. You can start with experiments. Have you ever thought of experimenting with words? For example: set yourself a goal to see if you can predict the emotions of others. Predicting an emotion means understanding it, and therefore it also means mastering it. Here, you can experiment with writing. Set out to write something with the goal of provoking a certain type of emotion in the reader. For example, write something with the intention of eliciting a laugh, or a pity, or a commotion, or an outrage. If the emotion you elicit is identical to the one you intended to elicit, you can say to yourself: I've learned to anticipate the emotions of others.

2) Remember that mastering emotions, while a huge accomplishment, is still not enough to become the master of your emotions.

Third week.

1) Listen to the messages your emotions send you. Take some time to listen to the coded messages of your emotions and interpret their hidden meaning. Each emotion acts like a physical symptom, or perhaps like a dream: it asks to be interpreted, sometimes to be avoided and sometimes to be tried again. Just as a negative emotion asks to be avoided, and a positive emotion asks to be tried again.

2) Write down everything that emotions have given you, or better write down somewhere everything that emotions have given to your personal growth. Too many times we leave unnoticed what an emotion has been able to teach us. We can't pretend to teach emotions without gratifying them. Emotions want to be recognized in their role as teachers, just as we want to be masters

of our emotions and be recognized as such. If a sequence of emotions has been able to transform you, educate you, or whatever else determines a path of growth in the positive or negative sense of the word, even if it's a painful experience: we are grateful to that sequence of emotions. And yet, in a second moment, make sure you move away from dependence on their educational role. While this is important, it's not essential: it won't be forever.

During the third week you will finally be ready to access the improvements in your emotional intelligence. After the several exercises that you will have done to understand the emotions of yourself and others, you'll be able to be aware of this understanding and above all to experience firsthand the beneficial and advantageous effects. In this sense, you will have to be active at the work or relational and sentimental level to put into practice all that you have learned during the exercise and experimentation with emotions.

During the third week, if everything goes as planned, if you're ready to be happy, to free yourself from the slavery of emotional automatisms that choose in your place when to appear and disappear, you will be able to consider yourself the master of your emotions.

Made in the USA
Columbia, SC
01 April 2021